D0897933

Moving the Goalposts

Why Maradona Was Really Useless...
How to Win a Penalty Shoot-Out...
and 65 More Astonishing Statistical
Football Revelations

Moving the Goalposts

**Why Maradona Was Really Useless...
How to Win a Penalty Shoot-Out...
and 65 More Astonishing Statistical
Football Revelations**

Rob Jovanovic

First published by Pitch Publishing, 2012

Pitch Publishing

A2 Yeoman Gate

Yeoman Way

Durrington

BN13 3QZ

www.pitchpublishing.co.uk

ISBN 978-1-90805-137-0

Typesetting and origination by Pitch Publishing
Printed in Great Britain by TJ International

CONTENTS

Introduction

I've read a lot about sport. I've read several books about cricket though I've never once attended a cricket match in all of my 40-plus years. I've read about baseball and athletics, about ice hockey and tennis. I've also read more books about football than I care to count. But, in all of these shelf-metres of books, I've yet to find a football book that satisfies my appetite for statistics and analysis in the way that Ken Dryden, Bill James or David Frith did with their respective sports.

While I wouldn't categorise myself as the bespectacled, dressing-gown wearing Statto of *Fantasy Football League* fame, the numbers behind and within sport, combined with a thirst for wanting to know why things happen the way they do on the pitch, make me closer to a football nerd than a lads' mag reader. I find some things that are written and said about football insanely frustrating, and it makes me want to shout in the face of the so-called experts to stop them spouting rubbish and misinformation. They may have played the game but they sometimes seem to know absolutely nothing about it. Having contained my irritation for so long I have now decided to do something about it, which is why you're reading this book.

I get irritated by people re-writing history. One well-received and supposedly definitive history of world football recently stated that Bob Paisley had John Barnes in his side for Liverpool, that Croatian legend Zvonimir Boban was a defender and that Stuart Pearce's *Italia 90* penalty miss was blasted wide. I only glanced through the book but knew (and have subsequently double checked for fear of falling flat on my face) that John Barnes signed for Liverpool in 1987 while Kenny Dalglish was manager (Paisley had retired four years earlier), Boban was a central midfielder and Stuart Pearce's penalty against West Germany went straight down the middle and was saved by Bodo Illgner's feet.

It did make me wonder what else was down in print as historical fact. Perhaps I'm being a little harsh, I know typos can creep into manuscripts, but what about some of the things decreed by the 'experts' as part of their TV 'analysis'? The analysis rarely goes beyond stating the obvious these days and the overseas guests at major international tournaments usually put their home-bred counterparts to shame. This dissatisfaction is a growing feeling among fans and even prompted a national daily to print a cartoon showing two testicles with microphones discussing a match. That catchphrase was pretty easy to decipher.

Early in Euro 2012, when Gary Lineker said that the Italian side wasn't [paraphrasing] 'like the ones of old in that they couldn't hold on to a 1-0 lead like they used to do', you just know I had to get my record books and calculator out (the results of my findings are printed elsewhere in this book).

While watching a Premiership match on ESPN I was listening to the comments of co-commentator Chris Waddle. He mentioned time and again that one side was keeping possession while the other was giving the ball away too easily. I wasn't sure that he was right because I thought the other side was passing the ball well. A few minutes later a graphics box appeared at the bottom of the screen showing that indeed, the team that Waddle thought was being wasteful actually had a successful passing percentage 20% better than their opponents.

There was silence from the commentators for a few moments and I actually thought my TV had lost its sound before the Waddler said: "Well, that's a surprise. You wouldn't have thought that by watching the game." But I, along with probably thousands of others watching at home, had thought exactly that. Why was it that someone who had played the game so well was unable to see what was happening before him? Do I need to mention what was said in my living room after the four wise monkeys on *Match of the Day* wrote off Andrei Shevchenko at half-time during Euro 2012 and he then went and scored twice in the second half? It's the closed shop mentality of some ex-players that grates. They played the game so they must know best is the attitude, but it's so often not the case.

But things are changing. Spurred on by the success of the book *Moneyball* in the USA, English football clubs are now analysing more and more aspects of the game. *Moneyball* told the story of baseball manager Billy Beane and his struggle to allow baseball analysis to take the place of the opinions of old-time scouts who 'knew the game'.

The result was a revolution in American sports and it spread across the globe.

Some younger managers in England have taken the *Moneyball* model and tried to apply aspects of it to football. They've had some success but once they come up against the Premiership it's pretty much a case of who has the most money wins in the end, no matter what small advantages you give yourself along the way.

The business of football analysis has come a long way. In 2003, Aiden Cooney, the head of sports data collectors OPTA, sent a copy of *Moneyball* to all 20 Premiership managers. He didn't get a single response. Now OPTA provides information around the world, every manager in the country has heard of Prozone (which tracks player performance) and everyone is looking to get an edge any way they can.

Purists, whatever that means, have argued that football cannot be analysed in the same way as baseball because the game flows. Well have they ever counted the number of times the ball goes out for a throw-in or corner, or is stopped for a free-kick? All of these stoppages mean the ball is usually only in play for about 60 minutes including any added time during any game. These stops and starts actually make it easier to analyse what happens at each re-start. That isn't to say that football doesn't have a high proportion of randomness (but then again so do many other sports), as Billy Beane says: "All you can do is put yourself in a position to benefit from the randomness."

Aiden Cooney tells a good story about this in relation to Liverpool buying Andy Carroll. "Glenn Hoddle said it took the striker six attempts to score a goal," he explained. "He used the stat as a negative, in fact if he'd bothered to study it, that gave Carroll one of the best ratios in the Premiership." At the time of writing, for whatever reason, Hoddle hasn't had a manager's job for six years. I'll be analysing his club and England record in the book.

Moving the Goalposts hopefully provides a refreshing look at the aspects of football that have previously been overlooked, ignored, taken for granted or just plain misinterpreted. It aims to uncover numerous hidden truths about the game and explain why certain myths survive to this day. For instance, do managers realise that corner kicks are less likely to get their team a goal than a throw-in? It looks at the undercurrents beneath a wealth of footballing stats. Are left-footed penalty takers inherently less successful than right-footers? Is it true that titles are decided in the games between the top four teams or relegation battles in games between the bottom six? What about the time off between games? Conventional wisdom tells us that a slightly longer break between games is favourable and we often see managers complaining that their opponents had an extra day's rest. But the truth is very different, the exact opposite of mainstream thinking. Do some footballing icons really live up to the hype?

The book is light-hearted in places, technical in others. It isn't always easy to understand, but that's part of the point. It doesn't make things difficult for the sake of it but, equally it won't be dumbing down the text or the ideas within it. In a previous life I was a research chemist where

I used what now seem to be primitive computer programs to analyse numerous variables that could influence a chemical reaction. The same principles can be applied to football and that's exactly what I've done.

I'll be trying to settle arguments once and for all. Who was the best, the worst, the most innovative, the most successful, the luckiest, the most unlucky? Who really were the greatest teams and greatest players? The book will also show that you *can* compare players and teams from different eras.

Over recent years statistical data has been used to analyse player and team performance. This book will show where this is relevant, where the data-gatherers have got it wrong, and where they're now getting it right; what is and isn't really important and why many traditional measures of the game are redundant; why certain methods of play do or don't work, and what is really required for a team to be successful.

A quick word here on the nomenclature I've used. I have generally standardised all games having two points for a win and one for a draw. Unlike many UK papers and TV channels that use win percentage as the percentage of games won (ignoring draws), when I use "win percentage" (Win Pct) it means the amount of points gained from the maximum possible available (using two points for a win). Simply put it's points won divided by points available. So if a team won four out of four it would have a Win Pct of 1.000. A team that won one, drew one and lost two would have a Win Pct of 0.375 (i.e. three points out of a possible eight). It's important to use the method I do because it takes into account draws and as two draws equate to a whole win it gives a better indication of a club's or player's record.

I will also refer to second and third tier to avoid confusion between the like of First Division, Second Division, Championship, and so on, which have all been used for the second tier of English football.

I have a healthy dislike of using friendlies in calculating win percentages, especially at international level. They are increasingly meaningless and often do not in any way reflect the abilities of the countries involved. England's 2012 win over Spain at Wembley is the perfect example. So I only use competitive games (European Championship and World Cup qualifiers and finals games for internationals and league and cup games at club level), unless otherwise noted.

The book is split into several broad areas of research such as league analysis, internationals, players and managers and these have been broken down into bite-sized discussions. I might spend more time than is healthy discussing why the second group games of a World Cup tournament produce most draws but on the other hand I'll find out whether Bill Shankly's top flight Win Pct (0.644) really puts him up there with the greats?

I know I'm not the only one interested in these issues. Just look at the ever-growing pages of statistics and tactical diagrams in the Sunday papers to see that there is a thirst for this kind of knowledge. This isn't a book which is meant to be read cover-to-cover in one go (though please do so if you feel so inclined), but it's something to pick up and flick through until you find something interesting, something that you hadn't noticed before. Read it and agree or disagree and argue about it, let me know (robj@innotts.co.uk) if you've disproved anything, proved it even more conclusively or have ideas for further exploration. I might upset a few people with my findings, but remember these aren't my opinions about players and teams, these are the historical facts. Many of these things have changed the way I look at the game and hopefully after reading this, you won't look at football in the same way ever again either.

Rob Jovanovic
Summer, 2012

Thanks And Acknowledgements

Among certain groups of my friends this book has caused lots of debate over the past few years. Hopefully it will do the same for you.

I'd especially like to thank Paul Camillin, Jane Camillin and all at Pitch Publishing for recognising what I was trying to do and going for it.

Along the way I've had input from many people, but I'd like to single out the following: Graham Palmer, Gino Farabella, Steve Hodge, Duncan Olner, Derek Hammond, Christoph Rabe, Uwe Baumann, Chris Barlow and Simon Jarvis.

PART 1:
THE LEAGUE

"I would not be bothered if we lost every game as long as we won the league."

– Mark Viduka

While 'soccer', a word derived in England, is often used dismissively as an unwanted Americanism, the use of league structures which are often thought to be a very British way of fairly producing a champion was actually an innovation 'borrowed' from either American football or baseball (depending on who you believe) in the USA.

It's the mainstay of organised football the world over and has been for well over a hundred years. It's been called the "bread and butter" of the football season, it's been described famously as "a marathon not a sprint" (or is it?), and while knock-out cups throw up bizarre one-off results, the league evens itself out over the course of 38 or 42 or 46 games and the best team sits atop it at the end of the season. From the humblest works five-a-side leagues through Sunday leagues and up to the millionaires of the

English Premiership it's the week-in week-out competition that is the constant throughout every football season.

Even when most teams spend most of their season with nothing to play for the fans turn out every week and many buy season tickets to watch in the most part meaningless games, at least in hindsight. Uefa deemed to called its premier competition the Champions League, though there is very little of a league involved in it and it's mainly populated by teams who aren't champions.

In domestic competition the league you play in is the most obvious status of your club, though some 'big' clubs occasionally drop down a division and small ones climb up them, even reaching the top tier, but usually not for long. The league structure is unforgiving and gruelling. I'll be looking at how quickly a league table settles into its final form, how you should concentrate your efforts to avoid relegation and what might help you get promoted. I'll be looking at which leagues have been the most competitive and when, what the life expectancy is of a club promoted to the Premiership and what the impact of using three points for a win has made. There will also be some history lessons, but no homework.

A Marathon, Not A Sprint
or
You Don't Win The League In September Do You?

"The league is a marathon not a sprint. It is where you find out if you are entitled to believe in how good you are."

– Bill Shankly

You don't win the league in September do you? Well, to get straight to the point, you might not be presented with the trophy, but the eventual champions are at the top from very early on quite a bit of the time. It might not be as bad today as in the 1970s or 1980s, but football managers and the media still tend to rely on a selection of clichés at various points of the season. One that often gets rolled out is that "you don't win the league in September". This is usually heard from a manager after an early-season loss against a perceived rival or after a TV game that has been hyped as make or break.

A sister cliché to this is the famous "it's a marathon, not a sprint". Both quotes lead to the same idea that the league campaign is a long one, and you have to go right to the end of May to win. Of course this sometimes is the case, and these exciting finales such as the one witnessed on the last day of the 2011/12 Premiership season, but these are the exceptions to the rule. The quotes do have some validity but are usually more relevant to the chasing pack. Though I haven't done the analysis I'm confident that many winners of athletics marathon races take the lead fairly early in the 26 miles. It's similar with football: more often than not the eventual champions of England have been proved time and again to have taken the initiative early in the season, as displayed here:

Month	%
September	35
October	50
November	61
December	69

The above table takes into account every top tier (First Division and Premiership) English champion from 1892/93 to 2011/12. The percentage figure shows the number of eventual champions who took to the top of the table by the end of the month in question. So, over the past 121 years, 35% of all champions have topped the table as early in the season as September. If you stretch the 'early season' to include October (by the end of which teams have usually played about a quarter of their games) then the percentage of table-topping champions reaches half (50%).

This figure rises to 61% by the end of November and 69% by the end of December. So, in the vast majority of seasons, we know the champions by Christmas. If you were a gambler it might pay to get your money on the leaders in October before the odds become too small. It would pay half of the time!

The biggest ever comeback was produced by Liverpool who in the 1981/82 season were 12th during the festive season after losing 3-1 at home to Manchester City on Boxing Day. At that point they had won only five of their first 15 games, but a stunning turnaround, helped by the newly installed three points for a win rule, saw them win 20 of their final 25 games to take the title. Going on such a run rarely happens these days. Six of the past eight (75%) Premiership winners have been top at Christmas and seven of the past eight (88%) were topping the table in October.

When those new season fixture lists come out take a close look at your team's opening games; they might make or break your season before it's even started.

A History Lesson

For younger readers, and those who have simply forgotten, it's time for a little history lesson. There was life before the Premiership. For most of my youth Manchester United were just a club that won the occasional cup and used to be quite good in the 1960s. They went over two decades without a league title. When I was growing up Liverpool were the dominant team, but there will be people now into their 20s who won't be able to remember a Liverpool championship-winning side. You might have parents or grandparents who talk about the Everton side of the 1960s or the Wolves sides of the 1950s. Few people alive now can recall Herbert Chapman's great pre-war Arsenal sides, but these clubs were all giants of the game. With only a small exception, most of the 92 clubs' glory days are behind them. Fans can only live in hope that they will return, or at least that better days are ahead.

Are the achievements of history any less because time has passed, because Sky TV wasn't there to cover it? Football has been organised for a century and a half and during that time teams have risen and fallen, dominated and then been pushed aside.

Here is a table of the 20 teams to have achieved the most points (at two points for a win) in the top flight of English football. If an all-time Premiership was to be formed, these 20 would have to be the founder members.

It's worth noting that almost half of the sides are no longer in the top flight and that the top ten clubs are pretty much the ones who have had the biggest crowds over the last century. Not for the last time in this book it's an example of money talking. I've also included a second table to show where the other current Premiership teams are positioned to give an idea of the number of games they need to win to reach the all-time top 20.

Most Points Gained in the Top Flight of English Football

		Years	Pld	Pts	Win Pct
1	Liverpool	97	3868	4537	0.586
2	Everton	109	4252	4521	0.532
3	Arsenal	95	3868	4473	0.578
4	Manchester United	87	3512	4191	0.597
5	Aston Villa	101	3918	4153	0.530
6	Manchester City	83	3344	3372	0.504
7	Newcastle United	81	3236	3328	0.514
8	Tottenham Hotspur	77	3128	3283	0.525
9	Chelsea	77	3132	3276	0.523
10	Sunderland	81	3150	3163	0.502
11	West Bromwich Albion	74	2880	2777	0.482
12	*Blackburn Rovers*	72	2720	2685	0.494
13	*Bolton Wanderers*	73	2802	2675	0.477
14	*Sheffield Wednesday*	66	2582	2572	0.498
15	*Wolverhampton Wanderers*	63	2422	2432	0.502
16	*Derby County*	65	2468	2397	0.486
17	*Sheffield United*	60	2356	2302	0.489
18	*Middlesbrough*	60	2400	2227	0.464
19	*Leeds United*	50	2060	2215	0.522
20	*Nottingham Forest*	56	2178	2149	0.493

Teams in italics are no longer in the Premiership

So any talk of a 'Big Five' (unless you talk in purely financial terms) shouldn't really include Chelsea or Spurs. The expected trio of Liverpool, Manchester United and Arsenal are in there along with Everton who have been in the top division longer than anyone else and also fifth-placed Aston Villa. The currently struggling Villa have spent a quarter of a century more than either of the aforementioned London sides in the top flight and have a better Win Pct too.

Of the other nine teams currently in the Premiership, but not in the above table, only West Ham and Stoke have a realistic chance of breaking into the top 20 anytime soon. The Hammers need another 51 Premiership wins to overtake Nottingham Forest and the Potters require a further 108.

All-time Top Flight Ranking of Other Current Premiership Teams

		Years	Pld	Pts	Win Pct
1	West Ham United	54	2206	2048	0.464
2	Stoke City	56	2144	1934	0.451
3	Southampton	35	1416	1319	0.466
4	Norwich City	22	902	826	0.458
5	Queens Park Rangers	21	860	804	0.467
6	Fulham	23	922	799	0.433
7	Wigan Athletic	7	266	219	0.412
8	Swansea City	3	122	114	0.467
9	Reading	2	76	65	0.428

The Worst Teams to Have Appeared in the Top Flight

Leyton Orient	0.250
Glossop North End	0.265
Darwen	0.268
Swindon Town	0.298
Barnsley	0.329
Hull City	0.336
Carlisle United	0.345

Just in case you were wondering about who has the worst top flight record in history, it's Derby County who managed only one win in 38 matches during the 2007-08 season.

Some of the teams in the all-time top 20 are there because they have stayed around for a long time without actually dominating any particular period. For every all-conquering Manchester United or Liverpool era, the list is also populated by the likes of Sheffield United or West Bromwich Albion. Conversely, some teams did dictate for a season or two, or even for a decade, but then they drifted down the leagues. So which team has dominated each decade for the past century and a bit?

In the early days it was Aston Villa and then Newcastle United that controlled the destiny of the championship and then the emerging Blackburn Rovers had their decade disrupted by the First World War. When official league football resumed in 1919 it heralded the era of one man, Herbert Chapman. First his Huddersfield Town side posted the best numbers of the 1920s (winning three titles but also being runners-up twice and third once) and then he moved to Arsenal where he produced an even more dominant side in the 1930s, producing the best Win Pct of any side during the first 90 years of English football. It's even more impressive when you learn that the 1930s were the most closely fought decade ever in the English game (see later).

Generally the league title has been the preserve of fewer and fewer teams since the Second World War, but the first two decades had some great title battles. The 1950s saw Manchester United and Wolverhampton Wanderers go at it head to head. Both sides won three titles between 1951/52 and 1958/59 but overall in the decade United had a slightly better Win Pct (0.620 to 0.605).

The 1960/61 to 1969/70 decade was a topsy-turvy one and seven different sides won the title. Ipswich, Spurs, Manchester City and Leeds all won it once while Liverpool, Everton and Manchester United each won it twice, but it was Everton's Win Pct that topped them all. Liverpool gradually took over during the 1970s and 1980s before Manchester United's complete dominance of the Premiership era. Their 12 titles in 19 seasons (1993-2011) tops even Liverpool's 11 in 18 (1973 to 1990).

Is Blackburn's dominance of the 1910s worth any less than Liverpool's glory years in the 1980s or Manchester United's in the 21st century? No, is the short answer. All are fading away into the history books and in 60 years' time Sir Alex Ferguson will just be a name on the page like Herbert Chapman or Stan Cullis. The important thing for fans of these great teams is to enjoy it while it lasts because, as strange as it may seem, you just never know when it will come to an end, and that sometimes happens quite abruptly.

The Greatest English League Teams by Decade

Decade	Team	Titles	Win Pct.	
21st century	Manchester United	6	0.751	*
1990s	Manchester United	6	0.730	
1980s	Liverpool	6	0.702	
1970s	Liverpool	5	0.690	
1960s	Everton	2	0.627	
1950s	Manchester United	3	0.620	
1940s	Portsmouth	2	0.586	*2
1930s	Arsenal	5	0.649	*3
1920s	Huddersfield Town	3	0.580	
1910s	Blackburn Rovers	2	0.565	*4
1900s	Newcastle United	3	0.599	
19th century	Aston Villa	5	0.620	*5

* covers 12 seasons
* 2 covers 4 seasons
* 3 covers 9 seasons
* 4 covers 6 seasons
* 5 covers 12 seasons

(Note: In the above table, decades start 1920/21 and end 1929/30 for example)

Saying Goodbye

It's a feeling that fans of fewer and fewer clubs now get the chance to experience. The last day of the season, a sunny May afternoon in short sleeves and brand new replica shirts applauding hands over head as your team, the new league champions, takes a lap of honour. There's the retiring legend with his kid on his shoulders, the beaming manager clapping the fans. You've seen it all on TV even if you haven't been lucky enough to witness it first hand, but you never know when it's going to end.

The fans don't know, the players don't know, the manager probably doesn't know, but it can just evaporate in front of your face and in some cases by the end of August, just a few short weeks away, that seemingly invincible set of players has fallen away and in some cases will never return.

Since the 1960s, the number of different league champions has been falling. Unless English football undergoes a seismic shift, the likes of Aston Villa, Nottingham Forest and Ipswich Town will never again be England's top club. Until Manchester City surged to the title on a wave of Middle-Eastern cash, there had been just three Premiership champions in 17 years.

Number of Different League Champions per Decade

2000s	3
1990s	4
1980s	4
1970s	5
1960s	7
1950s	6

It's unlikely that Manchester United will now drop back into mid-table obscurity and endure a championship drought like they did for the quarter of a century between 1968 and 1993. They have the finances, the players and the manager to continue challenging at the top for the foreseeable future. Their recent history has seen them capture a cracking 65% of the titles between 1993 and 2011.

However, Liverpool fans were probably thinking along the same lines when they were crowned champions in 1990. They had just won 67% of the titles over the last 15 seasons. What could possibly go wrong? Well, at the time of writing it's been 22 years since the once mighty Liverpool's last title, and realistically it's unlikely they'll win one in the next few years.

Arsenal are now closing in on a decade without a title and previous winners such as Leeds and Nottingham Forest have dipped as low as the third tier in recent seasons. It's a long road back and most teams won't make it to the top ever again. Here's a list of the clubs fading into the record books.

	Last Title	Years Since
Manchester United	2011	1
Chelsea	2010	2
Arsenal	2004	8
Blackburn Rovers*	1995	17
Leeds United *	1992	20
Liverpool	1990	22
Everton	1987	25
Aston Villa	1981	31
Nottingham Forest *	1978	34
Derby County*	1975	37
Ipswich Town *	1962	50
Tottenham Hotspur	1961	51
Burnley *	1960	52
Wolverhampton W*	1959	53
Portsmouth**	1950	62

*= now in second tier
** = now in third tier

Drifting Away

Nottingham Forest were relegated in the first Premiership season in 1993, Brian Clough's final year of management after steering Forest through 16 seasons of top flight football. It was a relegation that surprised the football world; after all it had been a spell that had seen the provincial side win the league title, two European Cups, four League Cups and they had never finished outside the top half of the table.

That summer the club produced t-shirts with the slogan "On Loan To Division One. Limited Edition for One Season Only". It was clear that all concerned expected this to be a temporary arrangement, and sure enough Forest bounced straight back up. Three seasons later they were relegated again, and this time the club didn't bother with the shirts. Forest again got immediate promotion but lasted just one more season in the top flight. They haven't been back to the peak of English football since. The glory years have been slipping away ever since and teenage boys now go to The City Ground who weren't even born last time the club was in the Premiership.

Almost all clubs that are relegated have plans for an immediate return to whence they came, but it rarely works out that way. In the last half century, most of the 'big clubs' such as Manchester City, Manchester United, Chelsea, Spurs and Liverpool have all been down and back but some 'big clubs' have been relegated and are yet to return. It's eight seasons and counting for Leeds United, 13 for Sheffield Wednesday and 14 for Nottingham Forest. Since 1962, 35 of the teams relegated from the top flight have failed to return. Your club might be next.

Relegated Clubs Still Waiting to Return

	Year Relegated
Bolton Wanderers	2012
Blackburn Rovers	2012
Wolverhampton Wanderers	2012
Birmingham City	2011
Blackpool	2011
Burnley	2010
Hull City	2010
Portsmouth *	2010
Middlesbrough	2009
Derby County	2008
Sheffield United *	2007
Charlton Athletic *	2007
Watford	2007
Crystal Palace	2005
Leicester City *	2004
Leeds United *	2004
Ipswich Town	2002
Coventry City *	2001
Bradford City *	2001
Wimbledon *	2000
Sheffield Wednesday *	2000
Nottingham Forest *	1999
Barnsley *	1998

	Year Relegated
Oldham Athletic *	1994
Swindon Town *	1994
Luton Town *	1992
Notts County *	1992
Millwall *	1990
Oxford United *	1988
Brighton & HA *	1983
Bristol City *	1980
Carlisle United *	1975
Huddersfield Town *	1972
Northampton Town *	1966
Leyton Orient *	1963
Cardiff City *	1962

* Been to the third tier or lower.

The Ultimate Question

One football debate which seems unlikely to ever go away is whether football is better today than in previous years? Are the teams better? Better is hard to define. Is it more competitive now than before, is it harder to win things? Despite the recent Manchester City versus Manchester United battle, the Premiership is getting more one-sided than ever before. The cliché of the rich getting richer while the poor get poorer is certainly true despite what the FA mouthpieces might have us believe.

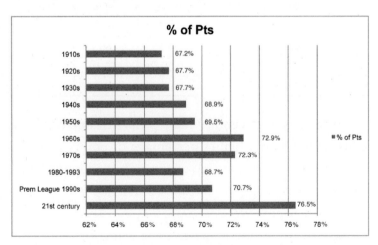

The graph above shows how the league champions have been winning a bigger and bigger percentage of available points. The dip in the 1980s was caused due to the introduction of three points for a win but after teams got used to the new points system the trend reverted to its previous course. The increasing strength of the teams at the top can be attributed to a build-up of funds by the top sides, who then buy the best players, even if many of them are then left in the reserves, and the cherry-picking of some of the best and most expensive overseas talent.

What about the other three divisions, are they becoming easier for the top teams to win? The answer is yes. Like the Premiership, the second, third and fourth tiers have all seen the champions of each level win a bigger and bigger percentage of points in the last 20 years, as shown in this table:

Table showing the % of points won by the Champions at each level by Decade

Tier	1960s	1970s	1980s	1990s	21st C
1	72.9	72.3	68.7	70.7	76.5
2	70.7	69.6	66.9	66	68.3
3	68.9	67.9	60.1	65.1	67.8
4	67.6			64.8	65.5

In the past half-century the top tier's champions have consistently won a higher percentage of points than the second tier's champions in an unusual development that filters down through the divisions, and it happens through almost every post-war decade.

So, since the war the dominant teams have become more dominant but how competitive is the league as a whole? Basically, in which decade was is hardest to win the league?

The Competitive Index

Without wanting to use confusing Greek symbols I needed to work out a straightforward method of comparing the competitiveness of each league. I wanted to have a simple measure of comparing leagues from different decades which would take into account the different numbers of games played in a season and whether two or three points were awarded for a win.

A basic, but telling, way of doing this is as follows. First, work out the percentage of points obtained by the champions and for the team finishing bottom of the table. By subtracting the latter from the former I got a figure for each division which I decided to call, for no particular reason, the Competitive Index (CI). The most uncompetitive league would see the champions win every game, 100% of the available points, and the last team lose every game for 0% of the points so the CI would be a maximum 100%. Conversely, the closest-fought league would see everyone draw all of the games and be equal on 50% and so the CI would be 0%. In reality most leagues are somewhere between the two, usually between 30% and 60%.

The chart below shows the CI average in each decade and illustrates how the top flight of English football has been getting less competitive since the Second World War, a direct opposite of the pre-war era which saw the league getting tighter and tighter.

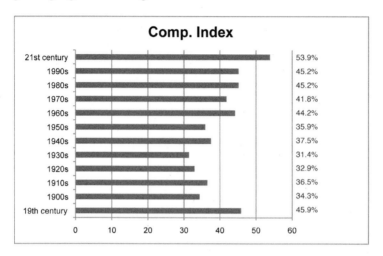

All of the most competitive seasons have taken place pre-war:

Year	CI
1937/38	19.0
1927/28	19.1
1901/02	23.5
1914/15	23.7
1938/39	25.7

Post-war, the most competitive seasons have been:

Year	CI
1974/75	28.6
1976/77	28.6
1991/92	34.9
1992/93	35.0
1967/68	36.9

The least competitive seasons have taken place most recently. In the 92 years between 1900 and the advent of the Premiership in 1992 there were just 11 seasons when the top flight had a CI of more than 50%, that is a season that wasn't very competitive. For most of those 92 seasons the CI was around the 35 to 45% range. In contrast, 11 of the past 13 Premierships have all had a CI greater than 50%.

Recent Un-Competitive Seasons:

Season	CI
2007-08	66.7%
2005-06	66.6%
2011-12	56.2%
2002-03	56.1%
2004-05	55.2%

The disparity has not only been exacerbated by the strong teams spending ever more to get stronger, but at the foot of the table we've seen some of the weakest top flight sides. Derby County set the new low for performance with just a single win during 2007/08 and Sunderland have had years of just three and four wins (2005/06 and 2002/03 respectively); is the year of a team doing an 'anti-invincibles' and going winless through a whole season coming soon?

So how does the ever less-competitive English Premiership compare with other leagues across the world? The table below shows how it was among the less competitive in the 2011/12 season. Scotland and Russia have leagues which split and see the top clubs play each other more often and the bottom clubs playing each other more often. More games between the top and bottom would most likely have widened the gap and increased the CI.

It's the three leagues often touted as the best in the world which have become the least competitive; the Premiership in England, La Liga in Spain and Germany's Bundesliga. Not only are these leagues relatively uncompetitive, but they have been dominated by a small number of clubs; Manchester United in England, Barcelona and Real Madrid in Spain and Bayern Munich and Borussia Dortmund in Germany.

	2011/12 season (or 2011 summer season)	
	Country	CI
most competitive	Brazil	35.1
	USA	38.2
	France	42.1
	Russia *	45.6
	Argentina	47.4
	Japan	50.0
	Belgium	53.3
	Italy	54.1
	Sweden	54.5
	Holland	55.9
	England	56.2
	Germany	56.9
	Scotland *	59.7
	Portugal	62.2
least competitive	Spain	64.0

* = unbalanced schedule

Two-Team Leagues

Uncompetitive leagues, dominated by a couple of the same clubs year after year? "It's like football in Scotland," is the oft-used put-down of continental competitions. But is the 'Scottish problem' really an unusual situation or is it actually the norm across Europe? We're led to believe that anyone can beat anyone and the exception proves that rule, but in the end it is usually the same two or three teams that win the title. The occasional upset sticks in the mind but rarely changes anything.

I decided to look at more than a dozen of the top European leagues and find out how varied their champions were. In half of the cases two teams had won the league for 75% or more of the last 20 seasons, but it's getting worse. When you look at the last ten seasons 11 of the 14 leagues have been won by two teams seven or more times and in nine of the 14 nations the % won by just two teams had risen in the last decade; a tenth nation (Scotland) stayed where it was at 100%. Most countries in Europe are being dominated by two teams and it's getting worse.

Titles won by Top 2

	Last 10 Years	%	Last 20 Years	%
Scotland	10	100	20	100
Portugal	10	100	17	85
Spain	9	90	16	80
Switzerland	9	90	12	60
Holland	8	80	16	80
England	8	80	15	75
Germany	7	70	15	75
Turkey	7	70	13	65
Italy	7	70	12	60
Russia	7	70	11	55
France	7	70	9	45
Norway	6	60	16	80
Austria	6	60	7	35
Sweden	4	40	8	40

dark grey = getting more dominant
light grey = getting less dominant
black = no change

Top two clubs in each country used in the table above as follows: Celtic and Rangers (Scotland); Porto and Benfica (Portugal); Barcelona and Real Madrid (Spain); Basel and FC Zurich (Switzerland); Ajax and PSV (Holland); Manchester United and Chelsea (England); Bayern Munich and Borussia Dortmund (Germany); Fenerbahce and Galatasaray (Turkey); Internazionale and Juventus (Italy); Zenit St Petersburg and CSKA (Russia); Lyon and Olympique Marseille (France); Rosenborg and Brann (Norway); RB Salzburg and Rapid Vienna (Austria); Malmo and Djurgardens IF (Sweden).

Mini-Leagues

The 'six-pointer' (or 'four-pointer' as it used to be called) has been part of the language of football for as long as I can remember. It refers to two teams in close proximity in the league playing each other. If your team can win it gets you three points and denies the opponents any and if the enemy were to win they'd get three and you'd get zero, a turnaround in the table of six points. The use of the 'six-pointer' in football punditry has spread to mean that teams in your vicinity, top or bottom, are playing more and more of these games to the point where the haves and have-nots of the Premiership are being split into mini-leagues. It's a mini-league for the title. A mini-league to get into Europe. A mini-league to stay up. A mini-league to qualify for mid-table obscurity. The list goes on.

The strugglers are deemed to have little chance against the teams chasing a Champions League spot so they should only concentrate on winning the mini-league within a league at the foot of the table. But does winning these mini-leagues really make or break your season?

At the top of the table the answer is no, or at least, very rarely. In 80% of the cases those super-duper Sundays don't really decide where the title is going, six-pointer or not. In 20 Premiership seasons, eight times the eventual champions have been so far ahead of the second placed team that they could have fielded their Under-10s and still won the title. A further eight times the champions have been strong enough and done enough against the eventual runners-up to keep them down in their place. There have only been four occasions (1995/96, 1997/98, 2009/10 and 2011/12) where the team that would have finished second actually overhauled the potential champions by virtue of the two games between them.

Most recently Manchester City took all six of the available points from their Manchester rivals to ensure that the two teams were tied on points and of course the blue side of Manchester won the title on goal difference. In 2009/10 Chelsea beat Manchester United home and away to clinch the title by a point; in 1997/98 Arsenal did the same, and in 1995/96 United themselves would have been two points behind Newcastle had they not beaten the north-easterners twice to finish four points clear.

At the foot of the table things have been much more interesting. Seventeen teams have been relegated because they didn't do enough against their fellow strugglers. That's almost one team every season. It isn't always just the bottom four or five that are involved in this particular mini-league though.

The mini-leagues below show the points gained between the teams listed in the abbreviated league table and illustrate how the league position of the relegated teams changed because of these matches. Sometimes these mini-leagues can bring in teams ranked as high as 12th in the table and sometimes the form of a team is turned upside down.

In 1993/94 Southampton narrowly avoided relegation because they gained 37 points against teams placed 1-14 in the table (averaging 1.32 points per game) but they managed only six points from their 12 matches against the six weakest teams in the division (averaging 0.5 points per game).

Complete capitulation against the worst teams around you is bound to spell trouble as Middlesbrough's three points out of 18 condemned them in 1993, just as West Ham's two points out of 18 did in 2003. Other times it is a remarkable run of good form against your closest rivals that saves the day like it did for Everton in 1994 when just 21 points in 26 games (average 0.81) was turned around with 23 points in just 12 games (1.92 points per game, a 237% improvement).

In the tables that follow, Other points = points gained from matches against the rest of the division and ML points = points gained in matches within the mini-league as listed. They show who would have been relegated had that team's 'normal' form continued against those around them.

1992-93 Position	Team	Other Pts	ML Pts	Pos	Team	Final Pts
18	Crystal Palace	41	8	18	Southampton	50
19	Middlesbrough	41	3	19	Oldham	49
20	Southampton	38	12	20	Crystal Palace	49
21	Oldham	38	11	21	Middlesbrough	44

1993-94 Position	Team	Other Pts	ML Pts	Pos	Team	Final Pts
15	Southampton	37	6	15	Tottenham H.	45
16	Sheffield United	31	11	16	Manchester City	45
17	Oldham	30	10	17	Everton	44
18	Manchester City	28	17	18	Southampton	43
19	Tottenham H.	26	19	19	Ipswich	43
20	Ipswich	25	18	20	Sheffield United	42
21	Everton	21	23	21	Oldham	40

1994-95 Position	Team	Other Pts	ML Pts	Pos	Team	Final Pts
12	Wimbledon	24	17	12	Middlesbrough	43
13	Leeds United	23	20	13	Leeds United	43
14	Coventry	23	15	14	Wimbledon	41
15	Southampton	20	18	15	Sheffield W.	40
16	Manchester City	19	19	16	Coventry	38
17	Q. P. R.	19	14	17	Southampton	38
18	Sheffield W.	19	21	18	Manchester City	38
19	Middlesbrough	18	25	19	Q. P. R.	33

1996-97 Position	Team	Other Pts	ML Pts	Pos	Team	Final Pts
13	Everton	34	8	13	Blackburn	42
14	Coventry	34	7	14	West Ham	42
15	Sunderland	28	12	15	Everton	42
16	West Ham	27	15	16	Southampton	41
17	Southampton	26	15	17	Coventry	41
18	Blackburn Rovers	24	18	18	Sunderland	40

1997-98 Position	Team	Other Pts	ML Pts	Pos	Team	Final Pts
13	Wimbledon	34	10	13	Newcastle	44
14	Everton	32	8	14	Tottenham H.	44
15	Newcastle	30	14	15	Wimbledon	44
16	Bolton	28	12	16	Sheffield W.	44
17	Sheffield W.	27	17	17	Everton	40
18	Tottenham H.	26	18	18	Bolton	40

2001-02 Position	Team	Other Pts	ML Pts	Pos	Team	Final Pts
16	Bolton	34	6	16	Bolton	40
17	Ipswich	33	3	17	Sunderland	40
18	Sunderland	31	9	18	Ipswich	36

2002-03 Position	Team	Other Pts	ML Pts	Pos	Team	Final Pts
15	West Ham	40	2	15	Leeds United	47
16	Aston Villa	37	8	16	Aston Villa	45
17	Leeds United	34	13	17	Bolton	44
18	Bolton	34	10	18	West Ham	42

2006-07 Position	Team	Other Pts	ML Pts	Pos	Team	Final Pts
15	West Ham	33	8	15	West Ham	41
16	Fulham	33	6	16	Fulham	39
17	Sheffield United	29	9	17	Wigan	38
18	Wigan	28	10	18	Sheffield United	38

Mini-Leagues

2007-08 Position	Team	Other Pts	ML Pts	Pos	Team	Final Pts
15	Reading	29	7	15	Sunderland	39
16	Birmingham City	29	6	16	Bolton	37
17	Sunderland	25	14	17	Fulham	36
18	Bolton	24	13	18	Reading	36
19	Fulham	24	12	19	Birmingham City	35

2008-09 Position	Team	Other Pts	ML Pts	Pos	Team	Final Pts
16	Middlesbrough	27	5	16	Sunderland	36
17	Hull City	24	11	17	Hull City	35
18	Newcastle	22	12	18	Newcastle	34
19	West Brom.	22	10	19	Middlesbrough	32
20	Sunderland	19	17	20	West Brom.	32

2009-10 Position	Team	Other Pts	ML Pts	Pos	Team	Final Pts
16	Wigan	26	10	16	Wigan	36
17	Hull City	25	5	17	West Ham	35
18	West Ham	25	10	18	Burnley	30
19	Burnley	21	9	19	Hull City	30

2010-11 Position	Team	Other Pts	ML Pts	Pos	Team	Final Pts
15	Wolverhampton W.	33	7	15	Blackburn Rovers	43
16	Blackpool	32	7	16	Wigan	42
17	Blackburn Rovers	29	14	17	Wolverhampton W.	40
18	Birmingham City	27	12	18	Birmingham City	39
19	Wigan	26	16	19	Blackpool	39

What Difference Has Three Points For A Win Made?

In 1981 it was decided that English league clubs would receive three points for a win, instead of the two points that had been on offer for the previous 90 years. The change was meant to promote attacking football, as teams would be tempted to go for the extra point on offer meaning more goals and less draws but, as usual, the game itself had other ideas.

In the old First Division, the average amount of drawn games during a season in the decade leading up to the change was 28.6% of the total. Initially the change seemed to work. The first five seasons using three points for a win saw an average of 24.6% of the games drawn. It was a modest reduction, but a reduction nonetheless. It meant that if you went to each of your team's 21 home games you'd be likely to see one less drawn match per season. This figure has risen slightly but remained fairly steady ever since (26.5% in the Premiership era).

The effect on goals scored was more pronounced, at least initially. Looking at all 92 league clubs, the goals per game average had been dropping since the open, attacking days of the 1950s. In 1960/61 we saw the post-war high of 3.44 goals per game. By the end of the decade it was down to 2.63 and by the 1980/81 season it had slumped to 2.47. In real terms this meant that if a fan went to all 21 of his team's home games in 1960/61 he would have seen 20 more goals for his money than if he'd gone to 21 games two decades later.

The first season of using three points for a win saw an instant jump to 2.60 goals per game and four years later this had steadily risen to 2.80 goals per game. However, the increase was only temporary and the average has been dropping ever since. The 2008/09 Premiership season saw the average drop back down to 2.47 goals per game, exactly where it had been during the last season of two points for a win. From the standpoint of promoting more wins and providing more goals, the change, with the glory of hindsight, seems to have been worthless. The same can't be said for the teams that have been affected along the way.

The new points system has been in place for 31 seasons and, as can be expected, there have been numerous changes in the league table because of this. It's stating the obvious, but where two draws would bring the same reward as a win, now three draws are required. Without wanting to bore you with every last positional change in the 124 final league tables in England since 1981, I thought it was worth looking at some of the major things that would have turned out differently if two points were still awarded for a win.

Perhaps surprisingly, the First Division /Premiership champions would have been different in only one of the 31 seasons. Blackburn Rovers would have been the one team to miss out because, with two points for a win in

1994/95, both they and Manchester United would have ended up on the same points, with United taking the title on goal difference.

It was also surprising to find that only one Champions League qualification place would have changed (Manchester City would have pipped Tottenham to fourth place on goal difference in 2009/10) and that only four different teams would have been relegated from the top flight. What was noticeable was that relegation dog-fights and the battles for European places would have been going on for longer during the season, thus making it more exciting for more teams' fans.

Outside the top flight the changes, if two points were still used, are much more numerous. In total, 67 different clubs would have had different promotions, relegations and play-off places thrust upon them, and some would have had very different futures as a result.

The most unfortunate of those clubs would be Cambridge United. In the 1992/93 season they were relegated from the second to the third tier of English football. But with two points for a win it would have been Sunderland who went down instead. Two seasons later Cambridge suffered the same fate and went down to the fourth tier, whereas it would have been Bournemouth going down instead. United briefly rallied at the end of the century but are now back playing non-league football.

Gillingham have had the most 'luck' with the three points system: previously playing for two points would have seen them miss out on a play-off place in 1987, been edged out of promotion in 2001. Nine different teams have been affected in this way on three or more occasions.

Maybe it's time to go back to two points. The seasons would be closer for longer, the affect on draws and goals scored would be negligible and some teams wouldn't have to wonder, what if?

The 1994/95 Premiership Table Using Two Points For A Win:

		PLD	W	D	L	F	A	PTS	GD
1	Manchester United	38	26	10	6	77	28	62	+49
2	Blackburn Rovers	38	27	8	7	80	39	62	+41
3	Nottingham Forest	38	22	11	9	72	43	55	+29
4	Liverpool	38	21	11	10	65	37	53	+28

How would history be changed if all league tables were retrospectively adjusted to three points for a win? With over 260 league tables dating back to 1888/89 you might think there would be quite a few changes, but there aren't. Further evidence that three points for a win changes very little at the top.

Not a single team would be saved from relegation using the new system, not a single league champion would be different.

The closest would be QPR who in 1975/76 finished a point behind Liverpool, but using three points they would have been level on points but still second on goal difference. In all, 13 divisional champions would change as shown below:

	Division	New Champions	Losing Out
1903/04	Two	Woolwich Arsenal	Preston NE
1911/12	Two	Chelsea	Derby County
1925/26	Three (South)	Plymouth	Reading
1949/50	Three (North)	Gateshead	Doncaster
1958/59	Three	Hull City	Plymouth
1963/64	Three	Crystal Palace	Coventry
1963/64	Four	Carlisle	Gillingham
1965/66	Four	Darlington	Doncaster
1967/68	Two	Queens Park Rangers	Ipswich
1970/71	Three	Fulham	Preston NE
1974/75	Three	Plymouth	Blackburn
1978/79	Two	Brighton & HA	Crystal Palace
1978/79	Three	Watford	Shrewsbury

Tight Finishes

Today, with all the hyperbole surrounding even the most dour of domestic league fixtures, it's easy to think that the most exciting football in history is being played right now. The multi-media, multi-camera angle coverage from non-league to World Cup can be overwhelming. The climax of the 2011/12 Premiership season was no doubt worthy of the excitement, but was it really the most exciting finish of all time as several outlets claimed? Surely the 1989 title match between the two teams going for glory head to head was more exciting. In some ways it doesn't really matter which one was, but it's important to know that it isn't the first time. Can you imagine the Sky TV meltdowns had these title race run-ins been screened simultaneously?

1949-50

After a terrific battle Portsmouth captured their second consecutive championship on goal average (goals scored divided by goals conceded) ahead of Wolves. The top three were separated by only a single point.

		PLD	W	D	L	F	A	PTS	GA
1	Portsmouth	42	22	9	11	74	38	53	1.947
2	Wolverhampton W.	42	20	13	9	76	49	53	1.551
3	Sunderland	42	21	10	11	83	62	52	1.339

Portsmouth won three of the four games against their title rivals and thumped Wolves 5-0 which went a long way to cementing their superior goal average. Goal average was later changed to goal difference (goals scored minus goals conceded), but more on that further on in the book.

1971-72
A dream for historians, this season saw Brian Clough, Don Revie, Bill Shankly and Malcolm Allison locking horns for the title. A single point was all that could be found between the teams.

		PLD	W	D	L	F	A	PTS	GA
1	Derby County	42	24	10	8	69	33	58	2.091
2	Leeds United	42	24	9	9	76	31	57	2.355
3	Liverpool	42	24	9	9	64	30	57	2.133
4	Manchester City	42	23	11	8	77	45	57	1.711

Manchester City led the league by four points in March but were overhauled in the final weeks. Unlike today's carefully choreographed finales, Derby beat Liverpool 1-0 to finish their season on 58 points but Leeds and Liverpool both had games left to play. Liverpool were held 0-0 at Highbury to deny them the title and Leeds managed to lose 2-1 at Wolves when they needed only a point to win the title on goal average.

Promotion And Relegation

With the vast amounts of money involved in the game today, the financial implications of promotion and relegation are greater than ever. They simply have the ability to make or break a club. It's true that the Championship play-off final is touted as the richest game in club football due to the rewards on offer for reaching the Premiership and these will grow even further. Wolverhampton Wanderers earned almost £40m when they came bottom in 2011/12 and that figure will balloon with the new 2013-2016 £3bn TV deal.

Over the years promotion and relegation has changed from one up one down, to two up two down and has now settled on three up three down in the higher leagues and four up four down in the lower ones.

The introduction of play-offs has meant that otherwise mid-table clubs can make a late charge for sixth or seventh spot, go on a good run and find themselves in a division for which they are ill-equipped. The disparity between tiers is of course most noticeable at the top. Was it always like this, and if not, how big has the gap become?

At the time of writing there had been 20 Premiership campaigns. During that spell, 50 clubs had been promoted in the leagues and 24 had been relegated in their first season (48%). Compare that to the 20 seasons before the Premiership when 60 teams had been promoted into the old First Division and only ten had gone straight back down (17%). The number being relegated immediately has almost trebled. But what of those that manage to survive that difficult first year, how do they do? Leading up to the Premiership the new-boys managed to make it into the top half of the table 21 times (35% of them), but in the Premiership era that's fallen to 22% and the last time it happened was over five years ago.

The following graphic illustrates the final placings of clubs promoted to the First Division, between 1971/72 and 1991/92. (Note in one season the team finishing 19th was relegated too).

Finishing Positions	Number of Clubs Finishing in That Position						
PRE-PREM							
1	1						
2	1						
3	2						
4	2						
5	3						
6	4						
7	1						
8	2						
9	1						
10	4						
11	1						
12	1						
13	3						
14	4						
15	6						
16	4						
17	4						
18	4						
19	3						
20	2						
21	4						
22	3						

The following graphic illustrates the final placings for clubs promoted to the Premiership between 1992/93 and 2011/12. The years indicate how long it has been since a first-year club achieved each position in the top half of the table.

PREM													time since
1													
2													
3													17 years
4													
5													11 years
6													
7													12 years
8													5 years
9													6 years
10													6 years
11													
12													
13													
14													
15													
16													
17													
18													
19													
20													

Life Expectancy

Paul Hardcastle told us that the average age of a US combat soldier in Vietnam was N-n-n-nineteen. Maybe he could write one about the average life expectancy of a team promoted to the Premiership and call it F-f-f-four. That's right, the average club is lasting just four years in the top flight before falling through the trap door once again. It's a problem that has been noticeable during the Premiership era and it's getting worse.

Not many promoted clubs are backed for survival and the chances of getting into the top half seem to be getting ever more remote as we have seen. Maybe a Leeds or a Sheffield Wednesday with massive support and some outside investment might be able to make a dent like Newcastle did in their second season back in 2011/12 but it seems unlikely. Does the position you gained promotion from make a difference once you're in the top flight and is it different to the old First Division era?

In the 20 years before the Premiership, the Second Division champions were relegated immediately on only three occasions (15% of the time) and they made it into the top half of the table ten times (50% of the time). However, since the advent of the Premiership it is more depressing for the newly crowned second tier champions.

They are now immediately relegated twice as often (30%, six times in the last 20 seasons) and have made it into the top half only five times (25%), exactly half the number of the pre-Premiership era. It's safe to say that the second tier champions are finding it twice as hard in the Premiership these days.

It's no surprise that teams being promoted as runners-up and the play-off winners are finding it even harder once they go up, but how much harder? In the Premiership era teams that have come up via the play-offs have been immediately relegated 13 times (68% of the time), while two more finished just one place above relegation. Below is a table showing the survival statistics based on the promoted team's position.

How promoted from 2nd Tier	1972-73 to 1991-92 Pre-Premiership Av. Years survived	Number of times lasted only 1 season 1972-1992	1992-93 to 2011-12 Premiership Era Av. Years survived	Number of times lasted only 1 season 1992-2012
Champions	8.1	3 / 20	4.1	7 / 19
Runners-Up	6.3	5 / 20	3.7	5 / 18
Third	8.2*	1 / 13	n/a	n/a
Play-Offs	1.8	3 / 4	2.3	13 / 19
Totals	7.0	13 / 57 23%	3.4	24 / 56 43%

* This figure is skewed because it includes Tottenham Hotspur who were promoted as the third-placed team in 1978 and have now been in the top flight for 34 consecutive years.

Nine of the promoted teams in the Premiership era are still in the top flight and so the average years survived figure will rise. History tells us that Swansea, WBA and QPR are unlikely to push the average years up by that much but the figure will rise a little.

Play-off teams have been known to come more than 30 points below the automatic promotion places and get up, so it's no surprise that they often come straight back down. In the last half century approximately 40% of the time the promoted clubs have finished in the same order in which they were promoted (that is champions finish highest, then runners-up and then third-placed team or play-off winners), a figure that hasn't changed in the Premiership era.

In the 20 pre-Premiership years, two newly promoted clubs went straight back down again only twice (and on one occasion it was when four clubs came up on the eve of the Premiership founding). Since then, two newly promoted teams have been immediately relegated seven times, and in one of those seasons all three went back down.

You might think that surviving the first season in the Premiership was the hardest part and that, if successful, you could build from there. However, commentators and pundits have started talking about "second season syndrome". This apparently refers to a growing number of clubs who have a decent first year in the Premiership before being 'found out' by the big boys and sent packing back down to the Championship. Is this a new phenomenon? Is it a phenomenon at all? Below is a table showing the numbers of teams that have survived the first year and been relegated in the second.

How promoted from 2nd Tier	"Second Season Syndrome" 1972-92	"Second Season Syndrome" 1992-2012
Champions	4 / 17	2 / 12
Runners-Up	0 / 15	3 / 13
Third	2 / 12	n/a
Play-Offs	0 / 1	2 / 7
Totals	6 / 45 13%	7 / 32 22%

Currently almost a quarter of teams lasting into a second season then go down, but three-quarters of them don't. This figure is 1.70 times higher than before the Premiership came along, but less than the likelihood of being relegated in the first season (which is 2.4 times higher now). It seems the "second season syndrome" is just a consequence of more teams being relegated again more quickly than before after any number of seasons, but maybe we should be talking about "first season syndrome".

Winning The Play-Offs

Does it matter where you are placed in the play-offs and is there an advantage to being seeded higher? In this section I'll refer to the teams as being placed A, B, C and D, with A being the highest seed and D the lowest. Over the years the play-off positions have changed from second to fifth to third to sixth in the current Championship and fourth to seventh in League 2, so this should help to avoid any confusion.

Some people have speculated that the team creeping in to the final play-off place might have some momentum that helps carry them through and others have wondered whether the highest-seeded team would be depressed at having just missed out on an automatic promotion place. Neither of these urban myths stand up to an investigation.

The tables below show the promotion statistics for each of the three Football League divisions and it's clear that the position from which the winning team comes is more likely to be the highest seed, A. It makes sense, this is the team that proved it was the best of the four teams over a long season and overall they go up 42% of the time, approximately double the figure of the next best seed, D (though B, C, and D are fairly even around the 20% mark). There is no big drop-off of teams just missing automatic promotion and the lowest-ranked team, D, is no higher than expected.

The only unusual thing about these figures is the performance of the second-placed team, B. It's the place that by far the fewest teams get promoted from in the Championship, only the third best seed in League 1 and the joint worst in League 2.

	CHAMPIONSHIP				
	Promoted	%	Finals Reached	%	% of Finals Won
A	9	38%	13	54%	69%
B	3	12%	10	42%	30%
C	6	25%	14	58%	43%
D	6	25%	11	46%	55%

	LEAGUE 1				
	Promoted	%	Finals Reached	%	% of Finals Won
A	8	33%	14	58%	57%
B	6	25%	12	50%	50%
C	3	12%	10	42%	30%
D	7	29%	12	50%	58%

	LEAGUE 2				
	Promoted	%	Finals Reached	%	% of Finals Won
A	13	53%	16	67%	81%
B	3	13%	13	54%	23%
C	5	21%	11	46%	45%
D	3	13%	8	33%	38%

	ALL Promoted	%	Finals Reached	%	% of Finals Won
A	30	42	43	60	70
B	12	17	35	49	25
C	14	19	35	49	29
D	16	22	31	43	37

By Far The Greatest Team

"And it's [insert your suitably-syllabled team name here, repeat], we're by far the greatest team you'll ever see." It's a song that's been sung for decades, mostly by fans of teams who are far from the greatest team that their opponents will ever see, it's more a declaration of undying commitment to the cause. But who, at club level, could really sing the song with any chance of it being remotely appropriate?

For this section I decided to try and deduce the greatest club side in English football history. Bill Shankly famously said "first is first, second is nowhere", so I've been through each league champion and worked out their Win Pct. Then I had to try and put each one in some kind of context because a team might win more games if they were playing against more weak teams, so I had to utilise the Competitive Index (CI) as previously discussed, for each season between 1888 and 2012.

The calculation I decided on was a simple one. I adjusted the CI from a percentage by dividing by 100 to get it into the same scale as the Win Pcts. Then I divided the Win Pct by the CI to give me, for want of anything better to call it, the Greatness Rating of each club. If two sides had the same Win Pct but one was playing in a season which was twice as competitive as the other, the side in the more competitive division would have a Greatness Rating twice as big as the other one. In plain English, the teams getting the most points in the most competitive seasons are the best.

I have compiled the 30 greatest teams in history by this method and the table is shown below. Despite having four teams in the top ten, it isn't Manchester United at the top, nor is it Arsenal, Liverpool or Chelsea. By my working, the greatest club side of all time is the Sheffield Wednesday side of 1929/30.

Top 30 Greatest All-Time Teams

Team	Season	CI	Win Pct	Greatness Rating
Sheffield Wednesday	1929/30	0.297	0.714	2.40
Manchester United	1999/00	0.430	0.829	1.93
Sunderland	1894/95	0.417	0.783	1.88
Tottenham Hotspur	1960/61	0.429	0.786	1.83
Manchester United	2010/11	0.413	0.750	1.82
Manchester United	1998/99	0.430	0.750	1.74
Arsenal	2003/04	0.500	0.842	1.68
Manchester United	2008/09	0.508	0.816	1.61
Everton	1969/70	0.488	0.786	1.61
Sunderland	1892/93	0.500	0.800	1.60
Liverpool	1987/88	0.504	0.800	1.59
Chelsea	2004/05	0.552	0.868	1.57
Manchester United	1993/94	0.492	0.774	1.57
Aston Villa	1899/00	0.470	0.735	1.56
Arsenal	1990/91	0.517	0.803	1.55
Arsenal	2001/02	0.517	0.803	1.55
Manchester United	2000/01	0.474	0.736	1.55
Manchester United	1966/67	0.464	0.714	1.54

Chelsea	2009/10	0.508	0.776	1.53
Nottingham Forest	1977/78	0.500	0.762	1.52
Blackburn Rovers	1994/95	0.492	0.738	1.50
Manchester United	2006/07	0.535	0.803	1.50
Aston Villa	1893/94	0.500	0.733	1.47
Liverpool	1985/86	0.508	0.738	1.45
Preston North End	1888/89	0.636	0.909	1.43
Manchester City	2011/12	0.562	0.803	1.43
Aston Villa	1980/81	0.500	0.714	1.43
Liverpool	1978/79	0.571	0.809	1.42
Leeds United	1968/69	0.584	0.798	1.37
Sunderland	1891/92	0.596	0.808	1.36

The 1929/30 Sheffield Wednesday team was phenomenal. At a time when the top flight of English football was at its most competitive (between 1926 and 1938 there were nine seasons with a CI less than .300 – meaning it was almost twice as competitive as in the last decade of the Premiership) they posted what was then the highest Win Pct of the 20th century. This table doesn't automatically mean that the 1929/30 Wednesday side would beat the 1999/00 Manchester United team which is the second best, but it means that at the time they played, Wednesday were ahead of a tougher bunch of opponents than United were 70 years later. But if the Wednesday players had had the same access to the training methods, equipment and nutrition that the modern era players had, there is no reason to think that they couldn't beat them though.

Elsewhere in the table, Preston's unbeaten team from the inaugural Football League season is only ranked 25th due to the poor quality of the opposition. The best of Liverpool's 1980s teams only comes 11th for similar reasons. Manchester United have the most sides included (eight), but if you're an Arsenal fan arguing about the relative merits of the 1991 and 2002 champions, you'll have to continue to disagree. Both teams had identical Win Pcts and played equally difficult opponents.

Apart from Preston (1888/89) and Arsenal (2003/04), the only clubs to have gone a whole season undefeated in a major European league are as follows:

Team	League	Season	Pld	W	D	Win Pct
Athletic Bilbao	Spain	1929/30	18	12	6	.833
Real Madrid	Spain	1931/32	18	10	8	.778
Perugia	Italy	1978/79	30	11	19	.683
Juventus	Italy	2011/12	38	23	15	.803

Despite the zero in the loss column, Perugia were only runners-up to AC Milan. The 19 draws cost them as Milan lost three games but still finished three points ahead.

Interlude: Mystic Meg

Predictions – Are They A Waste of Paper?

There could be a lot of money to be made if you could really predict football results and league finishes with any accuracy, but I don't see many poor bookmakers so I doubt anyone has cracked it yet. That doesn't stop newspapers and magazines printing pre-season and pre-tournament supplements filled with predictions of who is going to finish where and what they are going to win. It's really just a bit of fun, and equally I thought I'd have a quick look to see if any of them are any good, just for a bit of fun.

I looked at pre-season prediction tables and compared each one team-by-team with the actual final table that season. I gave each team one point for every place they finished away from the predicted place. So if a team was predicted to finish fourth and they came ninth in reality that team scored 5 points and I totted them up for the whole division. The lower the score the better the prediction. Here's how a few well-known publications scored, and just for comparison I also scored the league with the teams placed simply in alphabetical order and as chosen by my then three-year-old son, based on which badges he liked best. All highly unscientific I know, but I for one was interested in the outcome.

Predictor	Score
The Independent	40
FourFourTwo	45
The Guardian	46
When Saturday Comes	52
Three-year-old son	65
Mark Lawrenson	66*
BBC blog	76
Alphabetical order	114

* The ex-Liverpool and Ireland man predicted results each week during the season which is more difficult than simply listing them 1st to 20th in August, but in his favour he could see how teams were performing as the season progressed and adjust his predictions accordingly. His score is based a final table produced from his weekly predictions.

The Football Pools Panel
– Any Good?

In the age of online casinos, internet betting sites and the National Lottery, the Football Pools seem a little outdated. I can vaguely remember being at my grandparents' house on the occasional Friday evening when the Pools Man would knock on the door to collect that week's form and payment. The idea was to predict which games would end in a draw that weekend and points were allocated for home wins, away wins, score draws and non-scoring draws.

The game was initiated back in 1923, but a problem that never went away was deciding what to do in the event of postponed matches. In the early 1960s, during a period of particularly bad weather, the Pools companies decided that a 'Pools Panel' would sit and debate the postponed games and decide whether they would have been draws or wins. The panel was made up of ex-footballers and to this day includes Gordon Banks among others.

Wanting to know if the results decreed by the panel were any good, I looked at nearly 300 predictions spread over eight years from the late-1970s to mid-1980s. The panel had an overall success rate of predicting one of the four outcomes of 44%. The table below shows what percentage of their games were allocated to each of the four possible outcomes and how many they got correct in each result.

	% Predicted	% Correct
Home Wins	51%	62%
Away Wins	23%	38%
Score Draws	16%	21%
Non-Scoring Draws	10%	0.04%

In an average league season, the amount of home wins is usually in the region of 45%, so the panel probably predicted a few too many in that category, and the number of away wins is approximately 27% of the total, so they probably predicted a few too few of those, but the number of draws they predicted was broadly correct. The problem is that they were poorest at predicting draws (only a 21% success rate), so even though they predicted enough of them, they were allocated to the 'wrong' matches. It has always been a valiant effort, but goes to highlight the difficulty of predicting results on a game-by-game basis in the pre-Premiership era.

PART 2:
THE MATCHES

"We had Phil Dowd at Arsenal last year and we were denied three stonewall penalties so maybe he has it in his contract that he doesn't give away penalties against Arsenal."

– Paul Jewell

A major reason why football is the world's most popular sport is its simplicity. While an organised game needs a marked-out playing area, it can be played almost anywhere from back gardens to school yards to narrow streets in third world countries. You don't need any complicated equipment, just a ball. It can be large one or small one, boots or even shoes aren't necessary and the number of players per side can fluctuate from one to 100.

My earliest recollections of playing the game are split between a primary school yard where dozens of youngsters chased a single ball back and forth across the concrete, shooting at goals made out of huge piles of coats and sweaters, and of playing outside my house in games of one versus one, using opposing garage doors as noisy goals, much to the annoyance of the neighbours.

At the professional level everything begins and ends with a match. Each league season has the players taking them "one game at a time", cups and tournaments seem to be a never ending procession of matches, each one more important than the last.

To be successful you have to win them, but how? There's more to it than just sending out 11 players and giving them a ball. Today, a massive amount of preparation goes into a professional match. Tactics, training, nutrition, films of the opponents and computer analysis are all used to the extreme. But what of the 'match' itself? What is it about the time period between the kick-off and final whistle that is important to winning? How important is the venue, the number of shots you take, the number of passes you make, not just how many goals you score but when you score them, is it better to have a better defence or better attack?

Are there myths about these factors? Is a 2-0 lead really 'dodgy'? Does it pay to concentrate on your set pieces? The first thing to consider, as fans peruse the fixture list in August and are on the edge of their seats during cup draws, is where is the match going to be played?

Home Advantage

Most teams expect to win at home, or at least they expect to do better than when they play away. Why is this? The pitches are broadly the same nowadays, less are sloping or remindful of a ploughed field, there are still 11 players a side, etc, etc. Of course the fans, the familiarity of the ground, the lack of travel beforehand, the comforts of a superior dressing room, all tend to favour the home side. I've calculated the home advantage by taking the Win Pct achieved on the road (basically the games they'd win anywhere, anyway) away from the Win Pct achieved at home and shown it as a %.

Occasionally a team will perform as well away from home as they do at home, or even better, but this is the exception to the rule. The ball-park figure for home advantage is that there is a 20% improvement on a team's Win Pct at home compared to away. In the Premiership, it hasn't been Manchester United or Chelsea that have benefitted the most by playing at home but rather the teams listed below.

Home Improvements	
Fulham	28.5%
Newcastle United	26.0%
Southampton	25.9% *
Liverpool	23.3%
Tottenham Hotspur	22.4%
West Ham United	20.8%
Sunderland	20.6%

* includes The Dell and St. Mary's

As you can see, the cosy confines of Craven Cottage (Fulham), The Dell (Southampton) and Upton Park (West Ham) have proved beneficial to the home side that is used to them, while the vociferous support at St James' Park (Newcastle), The Stadium of Light (Sunderland) and Anfield (Liverpool) seem to have spurred the home side on more than most.

Even teams that struggle against relegation can perform reasonably well at home and often the teams from the opposite end of the table come unstuck on these visits. Even three of the worst teams in Premiership history, who each survived for just one season (Barnsley, Swindon Town and Burnley) had a combined home advantage of a whopping 29%.

How important is the actual stadium to home advantage? With brand-new stadia being constructed in recent years, I looked at some examples of home advantage before and after the move to a new home. Here are the current Premiership clubs that have built completely new stadia while in the top flight. Sunderland had only one season at Roker Park during this era which was deemed too short for comparison.

Arsenal	Home	Away	Home Advantage
Highbury	.634	.581	14%
Emirates	.772	.588	18%

Arsenal fans who long for the 'good old days of Highbury', which is where they regularly won trophies, might be surprised to learn that the Win Pct at the Emirates is much better than at Highbury (during the Premiership era) and the home advantage is greater too.

Manchester City	Home	Away	Home Advantage
Maine Road	.496	.363	13%
Eastlands	.655	.418	24%

While Manchester City's improved home Win Pct at Eastlands is no doubt down to having more money to spend on players, the away Win Pct is also improved for the same reasons. What is interesting is that Eastlands helps the team by almost twice as much as Maine Road did.

Southampton	Home	Away	Home Advantage
The Dell	.559	.299	26%
St. Mary's	.566	.309	26%

Notoriously intimidating for the visitors, The Dell managed to help Southampton to a 26% home improvement. Southampton got into difficulties after moving to St Mary's and were relegated from the Premiership in 2005. Even so, the new stadium managed to give them a 26% home improvement.

The moral of this abbreviated study is that building a new stadium will improve your home advantage, and even if your team gets worse it'll help just as much as the old ground.

For the 1981/82 season, Second Division side Queens Park Rangers ripped up the turf at Loftus Road and installed a plastic pitch. The following season they won the Second Division title and returned to the top flight. In those two seasons they had a home Win Pct of .821 and some clubs decided that plastic was the future. By the start of the 1987/88 season three more clubs had joined the Rangers 'experiment' – Luton Town, Oldham Athletic and Preston North End. The very nature of the surface, worries about an increase in injuries from the unforgiving surface, the difference in ball bounce, having to wear different footwear and so on led to calls of it being an unfair advantage. Here are the top flight home advantage figures for 1983-1988:

	Home Win Pct	Away Win Pct	Improvement
QPR 1983/84	.762	.452	21%
QPR 1984/85	.667	.214	45%
QPR 1985/86	.643	.238	40%
QPR 1986/87	.595	.286	31%
QPR 1987/88	.700	.500	20%
Luton Town 1985/86	.667	.429	24%
Luton Town 1986/87	.786	.357	43%
Luton Town 1987/88	.700	.275	43%

The average Home Improvement is around 20% in the top flight, and these two generally middle-of-the table sides regularly doubled that figure. Most of the top clubs of the era struggled on the plastic. Everton, Spurs, Arsenal, Nottingham Forest, Southampton and Manchester United had a combined Win Pct of just .329. Liverpool were the only side to thrive on the artificial surfaces by winning six of eight matches.

A new era of plastic pitches has been spreading in the 21st century. In 2003/04 Dunfermline, on a newly installed pitch, finished fourth in the Scottish Premier League and qualified for the Uefa Cup with a home advantage of 29% which was ahead of fifth-placed Dundee United's improvement at home of 21%.

Kicking Off – Can You Score Too Early In A Match?

In my younger years when I had a joint season ticket with my Dad, my team would usually win at home. Often we'd knock up big wins too, but if we scored right at the start he would often say "we've scored too early". This always confused me. How could you score too early? An early goal was the sign of a big win coming that afternoon, wasn't it?

To look into this some more I have analysed over 400 games in which at least one goal was scored. These were split between the FA Cup, League Cup, Champions League and Europa League. It wasn't rocket science to think that scoring first would give you a better chance of winning but I was a little taken aback at how big that advantage was. I found that teams scoring the first goal of a game have a Win Pct of .784.

Breaking down the times of the goals I further found that teams scoring between the sixth and 90th minutes have an even more impressive Win Pct of .801 but what happens when teams score in the first five minutes? Do they go on to win handsomely?

Teams getting the early goal actually won less of their matches. For goals in the first five minutes the Win Pct was 15% lower at only .647. Why is this? Does the team scoring so early then relax? Does the losing team change a possibly defensive formation and go for it? Maybe it's because teams who go a goal down early on have slightly longer to get back into the game. If this was the explanation then surely teams scoring between at between 6-10 minutes in to a match would also have a lower Win Pct than the overall figure of .784 because teams still had at least 80 minutes to equalise and win. But no, the Win Pct for goals scored at 6-10 minutes is a massive .891.

Below are the Win Pcts when the first goal is scored at various times, sorted by competition:

Score first goal	any time	0-5 mins	6-90 mins
FA Cup	.788	.563	.815
League Cup	.769	.600	.791
Champions League	.811	.769	.907
Europa League	.764	.750	.775
Overall	.784	.647	.801

How Have Rule Changes Affected Football?

It almost goes without saying that football today is a very different game to the one which developed 150 years ago. The introduction of a referee's whistle, crossbars and penalty areas as we know them have all affected the way the game is played while the laws of the game have gradually outlawed 'shinning' and handling. The future will likely see goal-line technology and eventually video replays.

The most recent innovation to have a massive effect on the game was the change to the back pass rule in the summer of 1992. Until then, a player could pass the ball back to his own goalkeeper who was then allowed to pick the ball up in his own area. The change meant that goalkeepers could not use their hands when the ball was passed back. Suddenly goalkeepers had to use their feet much more and the better ones could be used as a kind of last-chance sweeper behind the defence.

The 1992/93 season saw a succession of video funnies as keepers sliced hastily cleared balls out of play or got into trouble when they attempted to dribble their way out of danger. One team that suffered more than most because of this rule change was the league champions, Leeds United.

During their 1991/92 championship campaign, Leeds had often passed the ball back to John Lukic in goal and while he picked up the ball, bounced it a couple of times and then launched it down the field, the rest of the team would push up into the opposition half. Lee Chapman would try and win the ball in the air and the rest of the Leeds side would apply pressure in the attacking third of the field. But now Lukic couldn't pick the ball up and was having to deliver the ball downfield while under pressure and before the rest of the team could push far enough forward. The result was that Leeds' fall far from grace has only been exceeded by the Aston Villa side of 1899-1900. Below are the league champions who have had the worst season while trying to defend their title.

Champions	Season	Win Pct	Next Win Pct	Final Posn.	Win Pct drop
Aston Villa	1899/00	.735	.441	15th	29.4%
Manchester C	1936/37	.679	.429	21st*	25.0%
Leeds United	1991/92	.714	.464	17th	25.0%
Ipswich Town	1961/62	.667	.417	17th	25.0%
Liverpool	1905/06	.671	.434	15th	23.7%
Sheffield U	1897/98	.700	.483	16th	21.7%
Everton	1927/28	.631	.452	18th	17.9%
Chelsea	1954/55	.619	.464	16th	15.5%

* Manchester City were relegated having finished 21st.

The biggest change in the laws of the game, the one which had the biggest effect on how the game was played, was the 1925 amendment to offside. The change in the rule book only consisted of one word but it made a world of difference.

From 1863 until 1925 the offside rule was written such that an attacker was onside so long as he had three defenders between himself and the goal-line when a forward pass was made. At the time football was largely a game of dribbling and chasing the ball, with passing very much an unknown art and something done sparingly. The alteration in 1925 changed the word from three to two. Now only two defenders had to be in place to keep the forwards onside. The game was transformed overnight.

The FA voted to make the change because defenders were increasingly pushing up to catch the five forwards, which all teams used, offside. Games were descending into games of offside and the number of goals per game was dropping.

Goals per game in English football

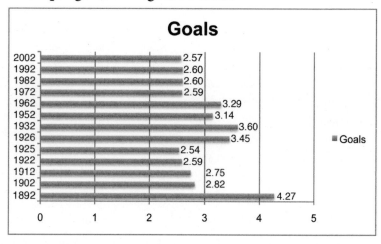

From 1892 to the time of the offside change, the amount of goals per game had dropped by more than 40%. The rule change reversed this trend immediately as the first season using the new laws saw goals increase by 36%. The goals continued to flow and the 1930/31 season signalled the peak of the goalscoring frenzy. Records were set that year for the most goals scored in the top flight (Aston Villa with 128) and the most goals conceded (Blackpool with 125). It was the biggest attempt to shake up the game until three points for a win was introduced more than half a century later.

A Game Of Two Halves?

There has always been something strangely romantic about the half-time break in a football match. In the very early years when teams played under different rules around the country, teams would sometimes play the first half using the rules of one team and the second half using the rules of the other. This led to some of the craziest games in history.

Half-time has always been the time to re-group, have a rest and for the losing team, work out how to turn things around in the final 45 minutes. How players try to achieve this has changed somewhat from the pre-war era of having a cup of tea and a cigarette, through the age of a slice of orange and a rub-down, to the modern age of energy drinks and looking at Prozone on an iPad.

The half-time interval has been the catalyst for some of the game's more enduring clichés and myths. Does a team really get a bigger advantage by scoring just before (or just after) half-time? Commentators often blather on that such and such a team didn't want the half to end, hinting that things wouldn't be the same after the re-start. Suddenly the team that was on the ropes would rise from the dead and miraculously turn it to their favour. The famous quote "a game of two halves" seems to reinforce this idea that the two halves of a match are almost disconnected and what happens in the first half won't have any bearing on the second.

While watching, and taking copious notes of, Euro 2012, I saw that of the 17 teams to lead a match at half-time, 14 of them went on to win and only three allowed their opponents to come back and draw, for a Win Pct of .912. Not one team managed to come back and win. It was more like a game of one half. No matter what the losing manager said or did at half-time, no matter how he changed his formation and no matter what substitutions he made, the games were largely done and dusted at 45 minutes. Was this tournament an anomaly?

I looked into the results of games, more than 400 of them, where one team was leading at half-time, including every match played at a World Cup finals and a range of Premiership and FA Cup matches. Here is how the teams trailing at half-time ultimately fared:

Pld	W	D	L	Win Pct
444	24	83	337	.148

Simply put, if you lead at half-time you'll get a Win Pct of .852 which for a 38-game season would give you 95 points.

In World Cup matches you might think that some of the scores may be more one-sided and that stronger teams might be more likely to come back in games where they were behind, but the results are remarkably similar. While considering every World Cup finals match between 1930 and 2010 the team leading at half-time's Win Pct is .848.

Only one team has ever come from 2-0 down at half-time to win a World Cup finals match in 120 attempts. The full range of half-times at the World Cup is as follows:

HT lead	Win Pct
1-0	.791
2-1	.837
2-0	.992
3-1	.967
3-0	.977
Other leads	.933

In the FA Cup a team leading at half-time has a Win Pct of .813. This slight drop from the other figures is likely due to the fact that teams from different divisions play each other and are slightly more likely to come back against a team one or two divisions below. That said, teams come back to win just 9.7% of the time in the FA Cup.

The Myth Of The Corner Kick

On a wet Tuesday evening in February, the crowd murmurs its approval as the home side pings a succession of short passes together across the wet turf and advances into their opponent's half. Then a player skips past a tackle and unleashes a shot from fully 30 yards. It hits a defender and spins in a vast arc. The crowd strains to watch the ball as it twirls and skids towards the corner flag. Will it be a throw-in or will it run for a corner kick?

The ball actually hits the flag pole and then rolls, slowly, out for a corner. The crowd visibly bounces as one in the seats and lets out a raucous cheer. Children clap, chants start up like a generator slowly growling to life and the bald-headed centre-half jogs forward to add his not inconsiderable frame to the attack. One coach is biting his fingernails, the other is barking barely audible instructions and waving his arms about. But why all the excitement?

Will it be played short, whipped in to the near post or lobbed over to the back stick? Will it be an in-swinger or an out-swinger? Will it be aimed for the penalty spot or pulled out even further to the edge of the area? Have they been working on something special in training?

The linesman watches eagle-eyed to make sure the ball is placed in the quadrant. The referee shouts at a couple of players who are pulling each others' shirts as they jostle for position. The goalkeeper stands on the line with his gloved hands held high, reaching for the sky. An attacker is standing just inches in front of his chest. Then the ball is struck and it fizzes towards the near post, right at the defender standing there who deflects it out for another corner.

The whole ritual starts again. Players jockey each other, the crowd edges slightly further forward in their seats and the coaches look on pensively. The ball is struck for a second time and it floats harmlessly into the area where the goalkeeper makes a comfortable catch. Home fans sit back, away fans jeer sarcastically and the game moves on. So why the excitement?

In the English Premiership, corner kicks bring a goal, on average, from less than 1.5% of all corners taken. So, very simply, corner kicks come to nothing more than 98.5% of the time. That is, almost every time. So why the excitement?

The only reasonable explanation for this waste of nervous energy that I can fathom is purely historical. Back in the day, the winger was an important member of every team and his crosses into the area would allow a hulking centre-forward to batter and bruise his way through defences and goalkeepers, putting the ball and player into the net if necessary. The good old English striker was expected to score a large portion of his goals with his head and, with goalkeepers receiving none of the protection that they are afforded today, he usually did so. Crosses from the byline or corner kicks were far more likely to produce a goal than they are in today's game.

The other reason for the excitement is perhaps because a corner does occasionally produce a goal and these deft flicks or thumping headers are far more likely to stick in the memory than the far more numerous failures. This was highlighted in October 2009 when Aston Villa scored from two corners in the same game to beat Chelsea 2-1. "Chelsea cornered", declared the *Observer* as they ran a table showing how many set pieces had been scored during the early part of he 2009/10 season. They missed the point though; the vast majority of the goals in their table of set pieces were not from corners, but rather from throw-ins and free kicks; the corner kick goal still proved to be a rarity.

So when will attacking players realise that they would have more chance of producing a goal by kicking the ball off a defender to win a throw-in, rather than skilfully manoeuvring their opponent into the corner before deliberately kicking the ball off the defender's shin to gain a corner? Scoring from open play after a throw-in is more likely to lead to a goal than a corner.

Team	Corners	Goals	Success
Arsenal	268	3	1.12%
Aston Villa	261	3	1.15 %
Blackburn	199	4	2.01%
Bolton	198	1	0.51%
Chelsea	237	2	0.84%
Everton	194	4	2.06%
Fulham	192	4	2.08%
Hull City	188	4	2.13%
Liverpool	271	5	1.85%
Man. City	212	2	0.94%
Man. United	260	4	1.54%
Middlesbrough	173	2	1.16%
Newcastle Utd	168	4	2.38%
Portsmouth	196	3	1.53%
Stoke City	178	3	1.68%
Sunderland	175	1	0.57%
Tottenham H	222	1	0.45%
West Brom. A.	232	3	1.29%
West Ham U.	191	4	2.09%
Wigan Athletic	217	4	1.84%

The above table shows each Premiership club's corner-kick success rate throughout the 2008/09 season.

During the 2008/09 season the Premiership produced 4,232 corners, which led to 61 goals, a conversion rate of 1.44%. For comparison, the same season in the Championship had 6,240 corners, yielding 96 goals: a 1.54% conversion rate.

Tottenham Hotspur, not known for their aerial attack, were the worst Premiership side at corners, while Newcastle United were approximately five times more likely to score from one. Bolton Wanderers, who, according to popular opinion, tended to play a long ball game and were successful from set pieces, were almost as bad as Spurs, and scored just once from almost 200 attempts. Since 1970 the amount of corners played short to keep possession rather than lumping it in to the box has dropped from 27% to 15%, why? Surely if the managers and players realised this they'd play it short more often wouldn't they?

The corner count in any game is still one of the few statistics regularly reported in the newspapers, but surely it's just a waste of time. Corners are included because they are very easy to count up and they *can* be used to see how much pressure a team exerted, and how much time they spent around their opponents' goal. But that can be misleading. A more accurate measure might be how many throw-ins the attacking side were awarded in the opponents' half, or even in the last third. And what does it all mean, even if you are relatively good at corners? Relatively speaking, Newcastle were by far the best Premiership side when it came to converting corner kicks into goals, but they only scored four times (10% of their total goals) and, guess what, they still went down.

Attack Or Defence?

It's the age-old question. What is it best to have, a great defence or a great attack? Some say that building a strong defence has to be the basis of any great team, others point out that attack is the best form of defence. To become league champions you need to be pretty good at both ends of the pitch, but which attribute has helped the champions most often?

Between 1888/89 and 1991/92 the league champions had the best attack 50 times (52% of the time) and the best defence 60 times (62% of the time). More recently, in the Premiership era, the best attack has tended to win out. In the early years of the Premiership the champions could get away with having the third, fourth or even fifth best defence but they had the best attack to go with it. Overall the Premiership champions have had the following:

Best attack	45%
Best defence	20%
Both	25%
Neither	10%

Twice Manchester United have had both the best defence and the best attack in the same season, and not surprisingly they won the title both times. In other seasons they have had the best attack eight times (winning the title on six of those occasions) and the best defence six times (winning the title three of those times).

Arsenal had the best defence four times in the first ten Premiership years but in these four seasons their best finish was second whereas in the second ten Premier years they were more likely to have the best attack. They combined that with the best defence for their last title in 2004.

The table below shows the final league placings for teams with the best attack and the best defence:

Season	Best Attack	Best Defence
1992/93	4	1
1993/94	2	4
1994/95	1	4
1995/96	1	3
1996/97	1	5
1997/98	3	2
1998/99	1	4
1999/00	1	6
2000/01	1	1
2001/02	2	2
2002/03	2	1
2003/04	1	1
2004/05	2	1
2005/06	1	1
2006/07	1	2
2007/08	1	1
2008/09	2	1
2009/10	1	2
2010/11	1	3
2011/12	1	1
Average position	1.45	2.20

In 2012 Manchester City became the fifth Premiership title-winning club to have both the best defence and attack. Despite ending the season tied on points with Manchester United, Roberto Mancini was quick to point out that his City team had scored the most goals and conceded the least. This got me thinking. What if teams were freed from the shackles of playing games based on wins, losses and draws and only competed in the 'pure' footballing way of trying to score the most and concede the least over a season? Points would be irrelevant in the table, it would purely be arranged on goal difference. Would a system like this change history?

Not that much would change, unless you are a fan of Liverpool, Newcastle United, Manchester United or Blackburn Rovers. The first two would have an extra league title in their record books, while Rovers would be stripped of one. Below shows the actual Premiership champions balanced against the ones that would have won a goal difference (GD) title:

Team	Real Premier Titles	Premier GD Titles
Manchester United	12	11
Arsenal	3	3
Chelsea	3	3
Manchester City	1	1
Blackburn Rovers	1	0
Liverpool	0	1
Newcastle United	0	1

The Balance Of Power

You might think that equal numbers of teams would have positive and negative goal differences, but the lop-sided nature of the Premiership table is further illustrated by the number of teams having a minus in their goal difference column (for the 17 seasons with 20 Premiership clubs):

Number of Teams With Minus GD	Number of Seasons
9	1
10	1
11	6
12	6
13	3

Over half of the time, 60% or more of the teams have a negative goal difference, caused by the smaller clubs getting thumped by the bigger ones and scrambling about among themselves for the rest of the time.

How To Score A Goal

It can be incredibly simple, it can be frustratingly difficult. Scoring a goal is the ultimate aim in football, though some negative thinking teams over the years might have seemed to forget this. The average Premiership team scores 48.6 goals in a 38-game season. These goals come from a range of methods in open play and various types of set piece.

These 48.6 goals are split as follows: 35.3 come from open play (of which 5.6 come from crosses), 3.1 goals come from corners, 4.5 from direct and indirect free-kicks, 3.4 are penalties and 2.3 are own goals. You can't do much about how many own goals the opposition will gift you over the course of a season apart from keeping them under pressure as much as possible and the number of penalties you receive can be influenced by how many times you get control of the ball in the opposition penalty box and by who referees your games and how they interpret many situations.

Some managers pay close attention to every little detail, including hours working on set pieces and free-kicks. As shown earlier, the corner kick is vastly over-rated and many Premiership teams only score one or two goals a season from hundreds of corners. Free-kicks, according to the press, play an ever more important role in the modern game. But as shown above they account for only 9% of the average team's goal output. If a team were to spend hours and hours to get a 20% increase in their free-kick efficiency that would only equate to about one goal over the course of a season. Surely the effort should go into scoring from open play where 73% of the average team's goals come from. A 20% rise here would send a team flying up the standings with another seven goals to their name.

> We've seen that corner kicks are vastly over-rated and, for the most part, nothing to get excited about. What about direct free-kicks? Are they over-rated too?

While at Manchester United, Cristiano Ronaldo was hailed as a world-class free-kick taker. Early one season during the Ronaldo era I watched Ryan Giggs being interviewed after a match. He'd taken a free-kick that afternoon and the interviewer asked if he still practised them on the training ground. Giggs, smiling, replied with words to the effect that he didn't need to any more because they had Ronaldo to take most of them now. In 2008/09 Ronaldo scored three times from direct free-kicks for United, the exact same amount as Chris Brunt scored for West Bromwich Albion.

Much was made of Andrea Pirlo's free-kick for Italy against Croatia during Euro 2012, as it was the first goal direct from a free-kick at the Euros for eight years. At the World Cup people expect to see amazing shots curl around the wall and into the top corner, usually from the boot of a Brazilian. Like many other parts of football history, the rose-coloured glasses have to come off to see the reality. There have only been 66 free-kicks scored in the 772 World Cup finals matches played between 1930 and 2010. That's once every 12 games.

World Cup	Games Played	Goals Scored	Free-Kicks	% of all goals
1930	18	70	1	1.4%
1934	17	70	1	1.4%
1938	18	84	0	0
1950	22	88	1	1.1%
1954	26	150	3	2.0%
1958	35	126	2	1.6%
1962	32	89	3	3.4%
1966	32	89	2	2.2%
1970	32	95	7	7.4%
1974	38	97	3	3.1%
1978	38	103	3	2.9%
1982	52	146	7	4.8%
1986	52	132	2	1.5%
1990	52	113	4	3.5%
1994	52	141	5	3.5%
1998	64	171	5	2.9%
2002	64	161	9	5.6%
2006	64	147	6	4.1%
2010	64	145	2	1.4%

The average is around 3.5 per tournament. The peaks at 1970 and 1982 just happened to coincide with two extremely talented Brazilian teams.

On the subject of penalties being awarded, the common cliché is that they "even out over the course of a season". A harsh decision against you this week will be balanced out by a "jammy" one in your favour down the line. While the law of averages does dictate that some teams end up getting as many penalties as they concede many teams have ended up with many more penalties going either for or against them.

The table below shows the amount of penalties received and conceded by teams that have been in the Premiership for each of the past five seasons (2007/08 to 2011/12). The "% in Favour" shows the amount of penalties awarded to that team out of the total number of penalties awarded in games involving that team.

	Penalties Received	Penalties Conceded	% in Favour
Manchester United	36	15	70.6%
Chelsea	34	18	65.4%
Everton	23	15	60.5%
Manchester City	31	22	58.5%
Fulham	19	14	55.5%
Liverpool	27	22	55.1%
Tottenham Hotspur	25	22	53.2%
Blackburn Rovers	26	24	52.0%
Aston Villa	28	27	50.9%
Arsenal	25	29	46.3%
Wigan	23	28	45.1%
Bolton	18	26	40.9%
Sunderland	19	31	38.0%

(Note: Only three of the other 16 teams to have played in the Premiership during the past five seasons have more than a 50% penalty share in their favour.)

So what effect does the awarding of more penalties to some teams rather than others have on the final table? I took, as an example, the 2010/11 Premiership season and looked at penalties scored and whether they had any effect on the final score of that particular match. If a side was 3-0 down and scored a penalty but still lost 3-1 it didn't affect the points total. If the side was 3-2 down and scored a penalty to equalise it improved their total by a point.

Taking into account the number of penalties scored, here are the numbers of points gained by them. I for one was surprised at how little difference they made.

	Penalties scored	Points gained
Arsenal	4	3
Aston Villa	4	4
Birmingham City	2	1
Blackburn Rovers	1	0
Blackpool	7	6
Bolton	4	1
Chelsea	6	4
Everton	3	2
Fulham	2	2
Liverpool	6	2
Manchester City	8	2
Manchester United	3	1
Newcastle United	5	3
Stoke City	3	0
Sunderland	4	4
Tottenham Hotspur	5	5
West Bromwich Albion	4	3
West Ham United	5	2
Wigan	2	3
Wolverhampton	3	2

Blackpool improved by six points but were still relegated, Spurs improved by five but were still six points away from a Champions League spot, Sunderland and Aston Villa would have had slightly different mid-table positions without their extra four points and Chelsea would still have qualified for the Champions League without their four.

In this particular season the awarding of penalties made very little difference. Of the 81 penalties that were scored, only 39 of them affected the score of that match meaning a gain of 50 points spread across the whole division. Breaking this down: On average 50/81 = 0.617 points gained per penalty scored, or each team improves by an average of 2.5 points per season.

The final 2010/11 table shows that 2.5 point leaps or drops would have changed very little. The champions and Champions League qualifiers would have remained as they were, and the Europa League place would not have changed hands. It is only the relegation battle that might have changed. With only two spot kicks, Birmingham City had one of lowest amounts of penalties awarded while Wolves, who finished just above them, had one more. Maybe another penalty in Birmingham's favour would have made a big difference to them.

Goals from open play tend to come most often when one team loses possession. Studies of international tournaments between 2006 and 2008 showed that 65% of goals came from a team winning the ball in its own half. Once they had the ball back, teams most often scored in under 20 seconds, mainly because the defending team was now out of position. The goals came so quickly because the attacking team made only between two and six passes in most cases before scoring. Possession was obviously a factor, but keeping the ball too long actually reduced the chance of scoring.

Does Possession Really Win Games?

Over the past few years there has been a growing discussion about possession of the ball during a football game. The England team is often criticised for failing to keep hold of the ball during the big tournaments while Barcelona at club level and Spain at international level are held up as examples of the triumph of possession football.

It should make perfect sense. The side that has the ball for longer should have more opportunity to create more chances and score more goals. The team without the ball will do more chasing, tire more quickly and have fewer chances to score a goal. The two combined mean the team with the ball will win all of the games, yes? No, not quite.

During Euro 2012, Spain started getting some criticism for the first time since they won the Euro 2008 tournament. Having captured the World Cup in 2010 they were looking to become the first team to win three consecutive international titles. Until the final their form had been patchy. A gritty draw with Italy was followed by an easy win over an outclassed Irish side. Then they came up against Croatia in a do-or-die final group game. Italy were expected to beat the Irish so a Spanish defeat against the Croats would be fatal. It was a chess match of a game with Croatia playing defensively for 70 minutes before changing formation and going for a decisive win.

For all of Spain's possession it was Croatia who created the most clear-cut chances and only a combination of some great Spanish goalkeeping and a poorly-placed referee prevented an upset. In the knock-out phase they stifled the French and spent the first 90 minutes passing sideways against the Portuguese before going on the attack in extra time and then winning on penalties. The talk before the final was split between those who claimed the Spanish were boring and those who said that the naysayers didn't understand and that this was the beautiful game. Neither were quite right.

Arsene Wenger summed it up quite nicely when he said: "(Spain) *have betrayed their philosophy and turned it into something more negative. Originally they wanted possession in order to attack and win the game; now it seems to be first and foremost a way not to lose.*"

Spain played with more attacking ideas in the first half of the final, but a 4-0 victory against a tired and ten-man Italian side didn't suddenly mean they had gone back to the team of four years earlier.

In the Premiership a table of average possession was released towards the end of the 2011/12 season. Arsenal were at the top with almost 60% average possession, followed by Manchester City, Chelsea and Manchester United. Next came Swansea City, a side that had won fans over with their passing brand of football, but their being fifth in terms of possession only translated into an 11th-placed finish in the actual Premiership table. This was very respectable for a newly promoted club, but they had failed to use their possession to maximum advantage. The problem was scoring goals as they managed only 44, which was 15th in the division. The other side of tiki-taka argument was Newcastle United, 11th in possession but fifth in the final table. Wolves were relegated despite having the ninth most possession, as they managed the third fewest goals. Goals win games, not possession.

This was never better illustrated than when Newcastle visited Swansea in 2011/12. Newcastle scored the first goal and won, as expected. They led 2-0 and won, as expected. They had only 38% of possession and won, not expected. Swansea also had the most shots but according to the BBC most of them were long-range efforts. Swansea had the ball but not could not be decisive with it. This might be an extreme example, but it happens much more than we are led to believe. Swansea failed to win 11 of their 19 home games that season despite a massive advantage in possession.

During Euro 2012 there was the inevitable 'group of death'. Actually there were two. The groups of Spain (first), Italy (ninth), Croatia (eighth) and Ireland, and Denmark (11th), Holland (second), Germany (third) and Portugal (seventh), were stuffed with teams at the top of the Fifa rankings. As previously discussed, Spain scraped through despite having a large advantage in possession, but the other group was perhaps more interesting.

Match	Possession	Score
Holland v Denmark	53-47	0-1
Portugal v Germany	50-50	0-1
Denmark v Portugal	58-42	2-3
Holland v Germany	53-47	1-2
Germany v Denmark	57-43	2-1
Holland v Portugal	58-42	1-2

Holland had the majority of possession in each of their games, on average 9% more than their opponents, but lost every time. In all the team with most possession lost four out of five times and in the fifth game, Denmark were denied a blatant penalty late on which could have produced a draw. Elsewhere in Euro 2012, the teams in Group A who had the most possession won only half of the games and in England's group the most possession won only two out of five times (the Sweden v France game was split 50-50). Spain aside (and Ireland too, because they were so poor), the group games saw the team with most possession win just six of 17 games. They also lost seven and drew four for a Win Pct of just .471.

The 2-0 Lead: The 'Dodgiest' Lead In Football?

When I started to look into this I wondered if this was the most misguided cliché in football, so I did a quick Google search. Sure enough there were people all over the world explaining how a 2-0 lead is the worst you could have. The argument usually goes: "But if the losing team gets a goal back the momentum changes and they usually equalise or go on to win 3-2." A recent game on ITV had Roy Keane at half-time saying that a 2-0 lead was "dangerous". Was there a comeback in that TV game? No. Is there ever a comeback? Very, very rarely. During Euro 2012 nine teams moved into a 2-0 lead, what happened then? Five times the game ended 2-0, twice the leaders moved further ahead (to win 4-0 and 4-1) and is that only unusual for the Euros?

Results for teams that had a 2-0 lead during European Championship finals since the current 16-nation format was introduced at Euro 96:

	Win	Draw	Lose	Win Pct
1996	9	1	0	.950
2000	10	1	1	.875
2004	9	0	1	.900
2008	10	0	1	.909
2012	9	0	0	1.000
Totals	47	2	3	.923

So, in the recent Euro finals teams recovered from 2-0 down to get a draw or win just 7.7% of the time, not exactly dangerous is it? How about at club level, maybe it's more dodgy for less-experienced club sides? I dissected over 400 matches at club level, both domestic and in European competition where a team went 2-0 up.

I found that 2-0 teams went on to win 94.4% of the time, losing just 0.3% of the time and being pegged back to a draw 5.3% of the time. These games ended 2-0 almost 27% of the time, and they won while scoring at least once more 61% of the time. The chasing team managed to pull a single goal back just 7% of the time. But even when a team did get pegged back to 2-2 it lost only 4% of those games:

Teams losing a 2-0 lead

Won by 3-2 or more	27%
Drew 2-2	69%
Lost 3-2	4%

Late Goals

It's seen as a sign of character, of having a never-say-die attitude, the late goal that saves a point or brings about a morale-boosting win. Down the years there have been numerous late goals that have changed history, from Michael Thomas for Arsenal at Anfield in 1989, Steve Bruce for Manchester United against Sheffield Wednesday in 1993 or Sergio Aguero to win the Premiership for Manchester City in 2012.

Do late strikes have much of an effect during the more mundane league fixtures during the season? Do some clubs have a knack for being fitter and therefore more likely to take advantage of a tiring opponent?

I decided to look at the Champions League, arguably the world's best club tournament. During the 2010/11 season there were 589 goals scored in the 212 qualifying, group and knockout stages. What effect did late goals have? Those inside the final ten minutes of normal time and those after the standard 90 minutes had expired?

I found that 59 goals were scored between the time of 80-89 minutes; this is approximately what you might expect if goals were evenly spread throughout a match. The 589 goals divided between nine individual ten-minute segments (0-9 minutes, 10-19 minutes, etc) would give 65 goals per segment, so 59 isn't too far off. What was more interesting was the fact that a further 34 goals were scored after the 90 minutes were up. This is even more surprising when you consider that stoppage time is usually in the range of two or three minutes.

Out of the 212 games, there were 60 score draws, with the final goal coming as follows:

Equalising Goal Time	Number of Goals	% of the Total
0-79 minutes	49	81.6%
80-89 minutes	4	6.7%
90+ minutes	7	11.7%

It shows that the desperate measure of throwing caution to the wind and piling forward in injury time does bring rewards as almost double the amount of goals came in the three or so minutes of injury time than in the last ten minutes of normal time.

Too Many Games

Premiership players today are the fittest and best prepared of any players in history. They travel to games in first class, they have people to deal with anything that they need and they travel in large squads of players. They don't have to play on muddy energy-sapping pitches, but we're often told by their managers that they play too many games, that the season is too long and that they need a rest. Do they really have a point, are today's players hard done by? I chose at random two teams to compare, the current Premiership champions and the 1978/79 Nottingham Forest team. Here's how the number of games measured up:

	2011/12 Manchester City	1978/79 Nottingham Forest
League	38	42
FA Cup	1	3
League Cup	5	8
Charity Shield	1	1
Champions League	6	9
Europa League	4	0
Competitive total	55	63
Friendlies	5	11
Season length	280 days	284 days
Players used	29	20

Both teams had to travel in Europe, Forest played more than double the number of friendlies and used a squad around two-thirds the size of City's. The lengths of the seasons were almost identical. Who would need more of a rest?

Playing Against Ten Men

The next bit of football wisdom that I investigated was the much-mentioned old chestnut of it being harder to play against ten men than it is 11. The thinking behind this one is that when a team has a player sent off they work doubly hard and cause problems for the relaxed team of 11 players who think they'll win easily now. Pundits will say that the combination of hard work against a complacent team will spring surprises. Well, occasionally they are right, but only very occasionally. After analysing 500 games from the 2010/11 season I found 69 that included a sending off. Below are the results of the team that lost a player:

	Red Cards	Wins	Draws	Losses	Win Pct
Home team	27	9	4	14	.407
Away team	42	6	7	29	.226

It's immediately noticeable that the majority of the red cards were issued against players on the away team (61% to 39%). An average home team has a Win Pct of around .600 so the loss of a player cuts this by a third and for away teams the average Win Pct is cut by about half from around .450. In no way can these figures support the ten men doing better than 11. In short, the away team is more likely to lose a man and they do worse when they do so.

Interlude: Chokers And Bridesmaids

Chokers, or, Bottling It – Thierry Henry's Goal Drought

Throughout football history there have been players who have had relatively anonymous careers but live on in the memory because of a single moment of cup final magic. Ian Porterfield, Bobby Stokes, Roger Osbourne and Keith Houchen are just some of the names that come to mind.

Conversely there are also great players who never made their mark in a final. Sometimes their team didn't reach many finals, if any, but some players have had numerous opportunities for glory and have, not to put too fine a spin on it, bottled it. One of these players is Thierry Henry, Arsenal's record goalscorer, a World Cup winner and a European champion. His league scoring record is superb, averaging over 0.5 goals per game over 16 years of top flight football. But when he's played in finals he has yet to score in ten attempts:

Club	Games	Goals	Average
Monaco	105	20	0.19
Juventus	18	3	0.17
Arsenal	254	174	0.69
Barcelona	73	34	0.47
Totals	450	231	0.51

Henry has played in numerous finals for club and country, often excelling along the way, but when the big day has arrived he has invariably failed to deliver. His record in finals is as follows:

Competition	Played	Goals
FA Cup	3	0
Champions League	2	0
Supercopa de Espana	2	0
Uefa Cup	1	0
World Club Cup	1	0
European Super Cup	1	0
Euro Championship	1	0
World Cup	2	0
TOTALS	13	0

While some say he's the greatest Arsenal player of all time and his league scoring record is superb, his contribution to finals is terrible. In fact he has less FA Cup final goals than Alan Sunderland.

Zlatan Ibrahimovic is arguably the most recognisable face of Swedish football, but he doesn't look 'Swedish'; no flowing blonde locks and boyish grin, the part-Croat, part-Bosnian is tall, powerful and an enigma. In league football he has been devastating, but in the big European and international games he's failed to deliver more often than not.

Recently he's better known for writing a much talked about autobiography in which he called Lionel Messi a "schoolboy" and exposed his falling out with Barcelona manager Pep Guardiola. Never that highly rated in the UK because he has famously failed until 2012 to ever be on the winning side against Premiership opposition, he has a sterling domestic scoring record in Serie A and La Liga (where he supposedly struggled but collected 16 goals and nine assists in 29 league games), winning numerous titles along the way.

He has also scored well in the group stage of the Champions League, which he's played in for 11 seasons, but when he reaches the knockout stage his goals dry up:

Champions League Record

		Group Pld-Gls	KO Pld-Gls
2001-02	Ajax	2-0	-
2002-03	Ajax	-	-
2003-04	Ajax	8-2	-
2004-05	Juventus	6-0	4-0
2005-06	Juventus	5-3	4-0
2006-07	Internazionale	5-0	2-0
2007-08	Internazionale	5-5	2-0
2008-09	Internazionale	6-1	2-0
2009-10	Barcelona	5-1	5-3
2010-11	AC Milan	6-4	2-0
2011-12	AC Milan	4-4	4-1
Totals		52-20	25-4
GPG		0.39	0.16

That's a drop in output of almost 60%. For Sweden at the World Cup, the biggest stage of all, he's similarly failed to deliver, and his record of no goals in ten games is puzzling. Including friendlies, he has 33 goals in 80 caps, for a very respectable international GPG of 0.41, and he's done well in qualifying tournaments, but as the 2014 World Cup may well be his last major tournament he's leaving it late to re-write his own personal history.

World Cup

	Qualifiers Pld-Gls	Finals Pld-Gls
2002	1-1	2-0
2006	8-8	3-0
2010	9-2	DNQ
Totals	18-11	5-0
GPG	0.61	0.00

Always The Bridesmaid – Never The Bride. Football's Perennial Runners-Up

While it's a cliché, it is true that football (like other sports, like life in general) can be cruel. For every cup winner there is a loser and for every crying finalist there are two more losing semi-finalists who never got their big day out. Supporters of many teams feel that their side has been unlucky at the last hurdle or that some ill stopped their charge which was out of their hands.

Some clubs seem to have an inferiority complex, "This can't be happening to us again?!" When some clubs win their fans seem to think that their route to glory was harder than every other winning side, "Why do they put us through this?!" TV pundits seem to think it's agonising to watch England play but look at the records of Italy before 2006 or Spain until 2008.

Domestically it has been Leeds United who, to outsiders at least, seem to have had a chip on their shoulder and Manchester City fans seemed to always think that they'd be jinxed in some way. For three decades and more, Leeds United have been known as the team that "should have" and "could have". Some of their fans still get upset about perceived injustices from the 1970s and in 2011 a book called *No Glossing Over It* was published about the wrongs that had befallen them. In some cases they may have a point but in others Leeds have just come up short. They didn't just lose big games when Don Revie was manager.

Who really are the nearly teams? Starting with clubs that just missed out on a league championship (I set the bar at a minimum of either three titles or five times as runners-up), I listed all the losing finalists and semi-finalists for the League Cup, FA Cup, Uefa/Fairs Cup, Champions League/European Cup, European Super Cup and Cup Winners' Cup. Then I worked out who had lost the biggest % of these games to be crowned the champion 'Nearly Team'.

Team	RU	CH	FASF	FAF	FAW	LCSF	LCF	LCW	ESF	EF	EW	Total
Leeds	5	3	4	3	1	3	1	1	4	4	1	80%
Preston	6	2	3	5	2	0	0	0	0	0	0	78%
Hud'field	3	3	2	4	1	1	0	0	0	0	0	71%
Sund'land	5	6	8	2	2	2	1	0	0	0	0	69%
Sheff W	1	4	10	3	3	2	1	1	0	0	0	68%
Blackburn	1	3	10	2	6	5	0	1	0	0	0	68%
Everton	7	9	11	8	5	2	2	0	0	0	1	67%
Wolves	5	3	6	4	4	1	0	2	0	1	0	65%
Chelsea	4	4	9	4	7	4	2	4	7	1	4	62%
Arsenal	8	13	9	7	10	7	5	2	1	5	1	62%
A Villa	10	7	10	3	7	5	3	5	1	1	2	61%
Newcastle	2	4	4	7	6	0	1	0	1	0	1	58%
Man C	3	3	2	4	5	3	1	2	1	0	1	56%
Liverpool	12	18	9	7	7	3	2	8	5	7	10	55%
Man Utd	15	19	9	7	11	4	4	4	9	4	7	44%

Note: The table shows the following:

RU   the number of times they have been runners-up

CH   the number of league championships

FA   FA Cup

LC   League Cup

E   combined European competitions

SF   lost semi-finals

F   lost finals

W   finals won

Total   % of these games lost

Fans of Leeds, Preston and Huddersfield should perhaps look away now. These are the teams that have missed out on the most silverware with Leeds losing in 80% of their finals and semi-finals. The table might put a smile on some Manchester City fans' faces as you can see that their side loses less of the big matches than teams such as Arsenal, Chelsea, Everton and more.

PART 3: TOURNAMENT FOOTBALL

"If you never concede a goal you're going to win more games than you lose."

– Bobby Moore

Every other year you can see the little red and white flags start appearing on cars around the land come early May. Everyone knows what it means, it's a tournament year. With the Euros and World Cup alternating every other even-numbered year the country is saturated with football paraphernalia. Sticker books piled up in supermarkets, magazine racks filled with preview guides. TV and radio promos seem to run endlessly and until very recently, England's chances of actually winning are hyped out of all proportion.

With Fifa having 209 members and Uefa 53 members, most nations have very little chance of even qualifying for the finals of a tournament, let alone winning it. With only one trophy up for grabs every two years a more realistic measure of success is to reach the quarter-finals of the World Cup, putting you in the top 4% of world football, or the semi-finals of the European Championship, meaning you are in the best 8% of football's most competitive continent.

With these tournaments getting so much media coverage, so many newspaper pages to cram and television hours to fill, every aspect is dissected. Fifa rankings are criticised and said to be unrealistic, the strengths of each group are weighed up and results charts published where you can plot England's route to the final or predict where they will lose on penalties. It all gives me great scope to investigate what's going on inside these great events.

Speaking on the BBC at the start of Euro 2012, Alan Hansen suggested that the latter stages would be filled by the "usual suspects". He meant the likes of Spain, Germany and Holland, but who are the real usual suspects in 21st century tournament football? There are other questions too. Do the teams from one continent favour playing against another? Are there any meaningless games at the ends of the group stage? How big an advantage do host nations get? And, of course, how do you win a penalty shoot-out?

The Long Road – Qualifying

Qualifying for the big tournaments takes the best part of two years and starts a few short months after the previous summer's exertions have ended. Groups often have ten games for each side with the possibility of two more play-off matches and that's with the World Cup now extended to 32 teams and the Euros growing to 24.

From a European perspective I compiled a table of qualifying success for the top 25 nations covering their all-time World Cup and European Championship campaigns.

		Qualified	*Entered*	*%*
1	Germany	21	25	84
2	Croatia	7	9	78
3	Italy	19	26	73
4	Spain	20	29	69
5	England	18	27	67
6	Czech	6	9	67
7	Denmark	13	20	65
8	France	15	26	58
9	Holland	15	29	52
10	Russia	4	10	40
11	Sweden	11	28	39
12	Belgium	10	29	35
13	Portugal	10	29	35
14	Scotland	10	30	33
15	Slovenia	3	9	33
16	Bulgaria	9	30	30
17	Romania	8	30	27
18	Switzerland	7	28	25
19	Poland	7	29	24
20	Hungary	7	30	23
21	Austria	6	29	21
22	Greece	6	30	20
23	Turkey	5	30	17
24	Ireland	5	30	17
25	Norway	4	30	13

The increase in European qualifying games has come from the break-up of various countries into numerous new nations. Two of these, Croatia and the Czech Republic, are now populating the top six qualifiers and the likes of Denmark are ahead of France and Holland.

In World Cups it's always the European teams that are listed as the favourites, with two South American nations in the mix. With seven World Cups between them, have Argentina and Brazil been consistently the best South American nations? South America has ten nations competing for up to five World Cup places and they battle in out through one ten-team league. The table below shows the five countries to have qualified the most times from South America since the war.

	Times qual*	1950s	1960s	1970s	1980s	1990s	21st C	Wins
Brazil	16	.792	.722	.828	.861	.783	.704	5
Argentina	13	.500	.731	.571	.735	.618	.687	2
Uruguay	9	.791	.654	.476	.545	.531	.523	1
Paraguay	7	.538	.333	.607	.417	.583	.561	0
Chile	6	.125	.538	.536	.600	.542	.474	0

* includes the times as hosts and holders too.

The Win Pct by decade includes both qualifying and finals results. Surprisingly Brazil were at their peak during the 1970s and 1980s while they were in the midst of a 24-year drought between World Cup wins. Argentina have been consistently inconsistent and Uruguay have been on a downward slope which was only propped up slightly by their good showing at the 2010 World Cup.

The South American Championship, now known as the Copa America and including guest CONCACAF teams, gives an interesting view of how certain nations have fluctuated. For instance, in the table below, showing each nation's Win Pct by decade, Argentina were only the eighth best side in the 1970s but managed to win a controversial World Cup on home soil and were only fifth best during the 1980s when they added a second in Mexico. Venezuela have made great improvements in this century but are yet to secure a World Cup finals berth while Peru and Chile are stuck in a two-decade long slump.

	1950s	1960s	1970s	1980s	1990s	21st C	All time
Brazil	.667	.417	.654	.706	**.771**	.750	.696
Argentina	**.788**	.682	.438	.567	.667	.750	.685
Uruguay	.625	**.900**	.500	.735	.476	.625	.619
Chile	.500	**.643**	.539	.625	.421	.455	.511
Colombia	.333	.125	**.654**	.583	.478	.615	.500
Peru	.487	.417	**.636**	.500	.469	.375	.479
Paraguay	.385	**.577**	**.577**	.450	.472	.423	.414
Bolivia	.167	.545	**.750**	.250	.500	.278	.389
Ecuador	.143	.313	.188	.350	**.500**	.150	.264
Venezuela	-	.200	.125	.100	.038	**.563**	.183

Bold = best decade

Fifa Rankings – Are They Mickey Mouse?

Introduced in 1992, Fifa's world ranking system has been the subject of mockery and ridicule from fans and pundits alike. It's sometimes easy to see why. Argentina, Holland and Germany have all topped the list while not being World Cup winners. Israel once reached 15th and Norway second. Neither had won, or even reached the late stages of a tournament.

Initially the system took into account matches over the previous eight years, but this was shortened to the present system of four years and each game is marked on the final score and quality of the opposition. The status of the game (friendly, qualifier, finals match) is also included in the calculation.

The rankings are used when drawing qualifying and finals groups but are they a good indicator of who will win during a tournament? I went back and looked at the Fifa rankings at the beginning of each of the World Cups and European Championships since the rankings were introduced. In each preliminary round group I looked to see if either of the higher ranked teams were eliminated and in the knockout phases whether any of the higher 'seeds' were sent packing. I didn't count games which went to a penalty shoot-out because I don't think Fifa rankings can take into account those special sets of circumstances.

I worked out the % of upsets and then, to give Fifa a break, I did it all again but discounted any games that were played between teams within five ranking places of each other. I thought that teams ranked, say, ten and 14 could probably beat each other on any given day and that the ranking couldn't be expected to correctly predict every one of those games. Here's what I found out for the World Cup:

	Group	> 5	KO	> 5	Overall	> 5
WC 2010	31%	25%	13%	7%	23%	16%
WC 2006	38%	38%	40%	8%	39%	25%
WC 2002	25%	19%	20%	20%	23%	19%
WC 1998	25%	19%	47%	21%	35%	20%
WC 1994	19%	19%	20%	7%	19%	13%

Concentrating on the figures given, which discount games between teams within five ranking points, the group stage caused more upsets (20% average) than the knockout phase (13%) and since the scoring system was revamped in 2006 these figures are lower.

In the Euros, the upsets are more likely in the groups but less likely in the knockouts, especially if you take out the 2004 performance by Greece (they drop to 9%). The Greeks were a one-team wrecking machine when it came to the rankings but despite their comic-book run they reverted to closer to their true ranking afterwards despite getting easier groups to play in because of their points boost.

	Group	> 5	KO	> 5	Overall	> 5
EURO 2012	38%	13%	17%	0%	27%	7%
EURO 2008	38%	25%	17%	17%	29%	21%
EURO 2004	38%	25%	67%	67%	46%	46%
EURO 2000	50%	38%	29%	17%	40%	26%
EURO 1996	38%	25%	14%	0%	26%	13%

The other major consideration when looking at the rankings is the performance of the host nation or nations. Often they have not had many competitive games during the period leading up to the tournament and so their rankings have fallen (England were 24th at the start of Euro 96, Holland were 21st in 2000). These 'lower' teams cause upsets because of their artificially low rating and the fact that they are playing at home.

Hosts' Advantage

How much advantage does hosting the tournament actually give? On the plus side there is familiarity, less travel and more fan support. On the downside there is pressure and expectation.

Less than a third of World Cups have been won by the hosts. Six times it has happened, two of those were the first two, and then there was a spell of three out of four between 1966 and 1978 before France in 1998. Few teams have ever won the World Cup so it's perhaps unreasonable to expect the hosts to win it any more, but how much does their play improve? I looked at every host nation from 1930 to 2010 and compared their Win Pct while hosting to their Win Pct at the finals immediately before and afterwards.

The table below shows that four of the 20 hosts didn't manage to even qualify before and after and so their combined Win Pct of .763 when they hosted shows how much of an incentive it can be. Only Spain, possibly due to the weight of expectation, performed worse at home. Italy in 1934 also were slightly down (only because they won every match four years later) but won it anyway. Every other host has played beyond expectations with England, France and Japan benefitting the most. Maybe that's the only way England will ever win it again, and we'll have to wait for at least 2026.

		Host Win Pct	Adjacent Win Pct	Host Advantage
1930	Uruguay*	1.000	DNQ	n/a
1934	Italy*	.900	1.000	-.100
1938	France	.500	.500	0
1950	Brazil	.750	.500	.250
1954	Switzerland	.500	.500	0
1958	Sweden	.750	DNQ	n/a
1962	Chile	.667	.167	.500
1966	England*	.917	.438	.479
1970	Mexico	.625	.333	.292
1974	W. Germany*	.857	.583	.274
1978	Argentina*	.786	.363	.423
1982	Spain	.400	.563	-.163
1986	Mexico	.800	DNQ	n/a
1990	Italy	.929	.591	.338
1994	USA	.375	.000	.375
1998	France*	.929	.167	.762
2002	South Korea	.571	.333	.238
2002	Japan	.625	.083	.542
2006	Germany	.786	.750	.036
2010	South Africa	.500	DNQ	n/a

* Denotes won World Cup
DNQ denotes did not qualify

Emerging Africa?

Back in the early-1990s Pele was famously quoted as saying that an African team would win the World Cup by the year 2000. It's a prediction that has been held up in ridicule of the world's most famous ex-player. The trouble is, he never said it. "The newspaper said that," he explained. "I said that Africa produced a lot of good players and that as they went to Europe and learned more, they would get stronger. I said the African teams were already talented, and that they could have a chance. I said Africa has the potential, but I didn't say they were going to win."

Even if he didn't say they would win, they aren't showing much sign of getting better either. The Africans have been consistent in getting a single nation into the last 16 and it's the Asian sides that are slowly improving.

Last 16 of World Cups by Continent:

	Europe	S. America	Asia	Africa	CONCACAF
2010	6	5	2	1	2
2006	10	3	1	1	1
2002	9	2	2	1	2
1998	10	4	0	1	1
1994	10	2	1	1	2
1990	10	4	0	1	1
1986	10	4	0	1	1

Quarter-Finals of World Cups by Continent:

	Europe	S. America	Asia	Africa	CONCACAF
2010	3	4	0	1	0
2006	6	2	0	0	0
2002	4	1	1	1	1
1998	6	2	0	0	0
1994	7	1	0	0	0
1990	6	1	0	1	0
1986	5	2	0	0	1

Semi-Finals of World Cups by Continent:

	Europe	S. America	Asia	Africa	CONCACAF
2010	3	1	0	0	0
2006	4	0	0	0	0
2002	2	1	1	0	0
1998	3	1	0	0	0
1994	3	1	0	0	0
1990	3	1	0	0	0
1986	3	1	0	0	0

European teams have filled 10 out of 12 semi-final berths (83%) in Europe and 11 out of 16 (69%) when playing elsewhere.

The Continental Divide

It's a simple one this. Do the nations of any particular continent do any better or worse against those of any other specific continent? Do sides of a continent have an overall style of play that upsets the comfort zone? I looked at the progress of each continent at the World Cup since the enlarged format was introduced in 1982. Here is how European teams have done:

	Africa	S. America	Asia	CONCACAF	Totals
2010	.667	.625	.500	.500	.588
2006	.722	.600	.800	.857	.736
2002	.583	.429	.500	.500	.500
1998	.545	.563	.929	.833	.663
1994	.643	.458	.700	.600	.569
1990	.800	.458	1.000	.667	.635
1986	.583	.308	.833	.667	.500
1982	.500	.650	.900	.800	.708
Totals	.627	.505	.721	.685	.609

Within this time frame, European sides have always done well against those from Africa. Apart from the blip of 1990, the last two tournaments have seen them beat the Africans more easily than ever before. More worryingly, they have struggled recently versus Asian teams in Asia and Africa, while still doing well at home.

Europe has been gradually catching up with and then overtaking South America, who are always perceived as the biggest threats at a World Cup. The only hiccup in this progress was the 2002 Asian tournament and with European teams historically struggling overseas it will be interesting to see how they perform at the first South American World Cup for 36 years in 2014.

Africa versus the other continents at the World Cup:

	Europe	S. America	Asia	CONCACAF	Totals
2010	.333	.000	.500	.500	.325
2006	.278	.000	.500	.750	.353
2002	.385	.333	.500	–	.389
1998	.455	.125	.500	–	.375
1994	.357	.000	1.000	–	.350
1990	.200	1.000	–	–	.429
1986	.417	.000	–	–	.357
1982	.500	.750	–	–	.583
Totals	.367	.250	.542	.600	.376

African sides have played very few games against Asian and CONCACAF teams since 1982 (only 17 matches compared to 84 against Europe and South America). They have also been fairly steady against Europe, but it's against South American sides that the big barrier to their progression lies. When the next World Cup begins, no African team will have beaten a South American one for 24 years and on their opponents' grounds it will be a tall order to start doing so then.

South America versus other continents at the World Cup:

	Europe	Africa	Asia	CONCACAF	Totals
2010	.375	1.000	.900	1.000	.667
2006	.400	1.000	1.000	1.000	.647
2002	.571	.667	1.000	.500	.600
1998	.438	.875	1.000	1.000	.568
1994	.542	1.000	.500	.500	.588
1990	.542	.500	1.000	1.000	.595
1986	.692	1.000	1.000	.500	.735
1982	.350	.250	1.000	1.000	.429
Totals	.495	.750	.933	.821	.609

With Europe and South America usually vying for the World Cup it must be worrying for the likes of Argentina and Brazil that Europe has been beating them more regularly in recent years. With most of the South American players displaying their skills at club level in Europe there is no mystery anymore. Brazil for one, will hope to reverse this trend when they host the 2014 event.

Asian teams versus other continents at the World Cup:

	Europe	Africa	S. America	CONCACAF	Totals
2010	.500	.500	.200	-	.382
2006	.189	.500	.000	.000	.233
2002	.500	.500	.000	.250	.438
1998	.083	.500	.000	.333	.182
1994	.300	1.000	.500	-	.429
1990	.000	-	.000	-	.000
1986	.167	-	.000	.000	.083
1982	.200	-	.000	-	.083
Totals	.286	.542	.067	.214	.271

Asian football has come a long way, but still has a long way to go. South Korea and Japan are regular visitors to the World Cup finals but other than when they hosted the 2002 tournament, they have yet to make much of an impression. They produce reasonable results against African sides and occasionally do well against European ones, but have only one win against the CONCACAF nations and none at all versus South America.

CONCACAF nations versus other continents at the World Cup:

	Europe	Africa	S. America	Asia	Totals
2010	.500	.500	.000	-	.363
2006	.143	.250	.000	1.000	.192
2002	.500	-	.500	.750	.550
1998	.167	-	.000	.833	.350
1994	.400	-	.500	-	.249
1990	.333	-	.500	.000	.286
1986	.333	-	.500	1.000	.438
1982	.200	-	.000	-	.167
Totals	.315	.400	.179	.857	.347

Another continent that struggles badly against South America is CONCACAF. Despite sometimes having a strong Mexico team and an emerging USA side, they still have only two wins in 30 years. Domination of Asia is not going to help any overall improvement in the World Cup.

Dead Rubbers

Is a tournament game ever really meaningless? Even if your side has qualified from its group with a game to spare, should you take it easy in the 'dead rubber' and rest your best players?

As usual I went back to every group game in World Cup history, 1930-2010. I found 47 nations that had secured qualification into the knockout phase with a game to spare. The final group games played by these sides gave rise to 25 wins, eight draws and 14 losses, but did these results affect how they performed in the next knockout game?

Result in last group game	KO win	KO loss	Win Pct
Win	18	4	.818
Draw	5	3	.625
Loss	6	8	.429

As can be seen, winning your last group game gives you a great platform to go and win your first knockout tie, almost 82% of teams do this, but drawing or losing your last match leads to going straight out in the next round 50% of the time.

Like other football competitions, the game at World Cup level has gradually been getting more defensive with less goals being scored. During both the group and knockout phases the goals have slowed down but curiously while it used to be the case that the groups were slightly more cagey and the knockout rounds had more goals it's completely turned around with the knockout goals being ever harder to come by:

Year	Goals per game Group	Knockout	Difference
1958	3.50	3.82	+ 0.32
1962	2.71	3.00	+ 0.29
1966	2.42	3.88	+ 1.46
1970	2.54	4.25	+ 1.71
1974	2.63	2.00	- 0.63
1978	2.50	3.50	+ 1.00
1982	2.78	4.25	+ 1.47
1986	2.38	3.00	+ 0.62
1990	2.28	2.06	- 0.22
1994	2.58	3.00	+ 0.42
1998	2.63	2.75	+ 0.12
2002	2.71	1.94	- 0.77
2006	2.44	1.88	- 0.56

"One-Nil To The Italy"

Previewing a Euro 2012 game on the BBC, Gary Lineker fell back into the kind of lazy clichéd small-talk that irritates me. Paraphrasing what he said: "The Italians aren't playing very Italian-like, they've lost two 1-0 leads. In the past we'd expect Italian teams to go 1-0 ahead and then defend the lead until the end." It summed up a long-held belief in the UK that Italian football was based around defence and if they got a goal ahead they'd just defend it to the death.

Is it reality or an urban myth about Italians and 1-0 leads? Italy had led 1-0 against both Spain and Croatia during Euro 2012 but been held to a 1-1 draw in each case. Was this really the norm? I decided to look at every game played by Italy in the World Cup and European Championship finals between 1930 and 2012. They went 1-0 ahead in 63 of these games and in each case I researched whether they shut down the game to win 1-0, whether they were pegged back to draw, won by a greater score than 1-0 or whether they actually lost. Here are my results, by decade:

	Won 1-0	Other Win	Draw	Loss	Total	Pct 1-0
1930s	1	4	1	0	6	16.7%
1950s	0	2	0	1	3	0%
1960s	0	3	0	0	3	0%
1970s	3	1	1	1	6	50%
1980s	2	6	5	0	13	15.4%
1990s	5	7	3	0	15	33.3%
21st C	1	11	4	1	17	5.9%
Overall	12	34	14	3	63	19.0%

After looking at this I didn't know if holding 1-0 leads 19% of the time was a high or low figure. So I had to go through every 1-0 lead for every other game in this period and guess what? The rest of the nations going ahead 1-0 kept the score as it was 20.6% of the time. Italy, rather than being the archetypal shut-up-shop merchants, are actually below average at doing so. Should I send this to Mr. Lineker?

Extra Time And Penalties – Any Advantage To The Equalising Team?

What advantage, if any, does a team get by equalising and sending the game into extra time during the knockout phases? Does the team that gives up the lead suffer an emotional letdown while the other side has an extra boost?

Looking at the last 30 or so years, I checked which team scored the equalising goal and whether they went on to win or lose. In almost 70% of occasions the equalising team goes on to get through the round. Penalty shoot-outs dilute this effect somewhat, the record of equalising teams in extra time (with and without the Golden Goal) is an impressive 83%.

	ET	GG	ET + GG	Penalties	Overall
World Cup 1982-2010	5-1	2-0	7-1	7-6	14-7 (67%)
Euro 1980-2012	1-1	2-0	3-1	2-1	5-2 (71%)
Combined	6-2	4-0	10-2	9-7	19-9 (68%)

ET = Extra time
GG = Golden goal

How To Win A Penalty Shoot-Out

It should be one of the easiest things in football. Yet it has become one of the most infuriating, the cruellest, and most heartbreaking parts of the game. It's now firmly written into sporting folklore, yes, it's the penalty shoot-out.

Because the shoot-out is such a vital part of tournament football, various studies have been done but not the obvious one, the one using real high pressure data. Economists and university professors have looked at shoot-outs, but while they analysed the colour of the goalkeeper's shirt (with students shooting on a training ground) or whether the shooter chose left or right (which does have a little merit) they have failed to show the simplest rules to follow if you want to win in a shoot-out.

There has been much written about game theory and whether players should change the placement of their kicks and what goalkeepers can do to guess the direction of the ball. Goalkeepers already guess the right way more than half of the time and don't save many. Game theory is redundant if the shooter can hit the correct area in the top half of the net every time, then there's nothing a goalkeeper can do.

149

My initial study investigated every shoot-out in World Cup finals and European Championship finals tournaments. It covers 32 shoot-outs made up of 310 spot kicks spread over almost 40 years and through all of those tense moments the bottom line is this: in tournament penalty shoot-outs at the highest level the scoring rate is 73% or an average of 3.65 out of five penalties (in normal play during World Cups, the penalty kick success rate is 83%).

Based on this, in theory, if you score four of your five kicks you should win and that proved to be true in 22 of the cases, or 69% of the time. So to get to this level what little advantage can you give yourself to get ahead? Surely the tiniest edge could make all the difference and here are the ways that you can do this.

	World Cup		*Euro Champs*		*Overall*	
Total shoot-outs	21		11		32	
Total shots taken	200		110		310	

	World Cup		*Euro Champs*		*Overall*	
Shots scored	144	72%	83	75%	227	73%
Shots saved	41	21%	16	15%	57	19%
Shots missed	15	7%	11	10%	26	8%

Firstly, take the first kick if you get the chance. Teams that shoot first win 56% of all shoot-outs and that figure rises to 63% if the first team manages to score with the opening kick. So it's pretty disheartening to know that before you've even stepped forward your chances of winning could be as low as 37%.

	World Cup		Euro Champs		Overall	
	Number	*%*	*Number*	*%*	*Number*	*%*
Win if shoot first	13-8	62%	5-6	45%	18-14	56%
Win if shoot first and score	11-5	69%	4-4	50%	15-9	63%

Next, if you can, pick only right-footed players. Of all the penalties taken by left-footed players the goalkeeper managed to save 25% of them, compared to only 18% against right-footed shooters, that is a third more are saved.

	World Cup		Euro Champs		Overall	
	Number	*%*	*Number*	*%*	*Number*	*%*
Left foot scored	28	68%	13	69%	41	68%
Left foot saved	9	22%	6	31%	15	25%
Left foot missed	4	10%	0	0	4	7%
Right foot scored	116	73%	51	76%	167	74%
Right foot saved	32	20%	8	12%	40	18%
Right foot missed	11	7%	8	12%	19	8%

In these shoot-outs it emerged that 8% of the time the goalkeeper wasn't even needed because the shooter missed the target altogether. But lets assume the players do hit the target, whereabouts should they aim? Bottom left? Top right? Down the middle?

As is normal these things can be over-complicated, but with shoot-outs there is a very simple guide that can be followed to great success. Shoot into the top half of the goal. If you draw an imaginary line across the goal halfway up the posts you get the most important dividing line.

On-target penalties in the top half of the goal are successful a whopping 98% of the time. These shots don't have to be right in the top corner or just under the bar, just above halfway.

Now when you analyse shots into the bottom half of the goal the success rate of shots on target drops sharply to only 70% as the keepers save % rises from 2% to 28%. With these figures to hand, I'm surprised that only 37% of shots are aimed at the top half.

	World Cup		Euro Champs		Overall	
	Number	%	Number	%	Number	%
Top half scored	59	79%	32	80%	91	79%
Top half saved	2	3%	0	0	2	2%
Top half missed	14	18%	8	20%	22	19%
Top half if on target		97%		100%		98%
Bottom half scored	85	68%	51	73%	136	70%
Bottom half saved	39	31%	16	23%	55	28%
Bottom half missed	1	1%	3	4%	4	2%
Bottom half if on target		69%		74%		70%

So if you go first, pick your right-footed players and shoot above halfway you're almost certain to win, right? Well, almost. There are a couple of variables that can scupper these plans. One isn't as important as some people think, the goalkeeper. Goalkeepers guess the right way 49% of the time, but even when they do they only save 40% of those kicks.

The more important factor is pressure/incentive. It's been proved that if you step forward with the chance to win the tie with your kick it's a massive incentive. Rather than causing some players to choke these kicks have been successful an unprecedented 100% of the time. However when a player steps forward needing to score to keep his team alive the average success rate of 73% plummets to 50%.

	World Cup		Euro Champs		Overall	
	Number	%	Number	%	Number	%
Keeper guess right goal	43	49%	41	64%	84	55%
Keeper guess right save	41	47%	16	25%	57	38%
Keeper guess right miss	4	4%	7	11%	11	7%
Keeper guess wrong	106	53%	46	42%	152	49%
Keeper guess right	94	47%	64	58%	158	51%

	World Cup		Euro Champs		Overall	
	Number	%	Number	%	Number	%
SD to win	12-0	100%	8-0	100%	20-0	100%
SD to survive	5-8	33%	6-3	67%	11-11	50%

You should also be careful where you place your shooters in order one to five. In almost 60% of shoot-outs they are over in nine or less kicks. Maybe someone should have told Cristiano Ronaldo.

Finally, here is a fairly useless table showing the won-lost records of teams by their shirt colour:

Colour	World Cups	Euros	Overall
Blue	5-5	2-1	7-6
Grey	0-0	0-1	0-1
Orange	0-1	0-2	0-3
White	8-6	4-5	12-11
Red	2-4	5-1	7-6
Yellow	3-3	0-1	3-4
Green	2-2	0-0	2-2

Where have England gone wrong? England have now lost six out of seven shoot-outs. So what is going wrong? Other teams must be just as nervous. Other teams will have had the opportunity to practise the same amount as England. The cruel, but true answer, is that almost every aspect of England's shoot-out statistics are inferior.

Goalkeepers have little to lose, they are expected to let most penalties in, but if they manage to save one they can be the unexpected hero. England's goalkeepers have actually managed to guess the right way 21 times, 58% of the time, which is far above the average for the other sides of 50%. However they have only managed to make two saves in seven shoot-outs. This 7% save percentage is way below the other teams' average of 30%. A couple more saves here and there would take a massive amount of pressure off the shooters.

England don't take advantage of going first. Though they won for the only time when shooting first, they have lost three others, a 25% success rate compared to 61% for everyone else.

The shooting record is:

Penalties	Scored	Saved	Missed	Goal%
35	23	9	3	66%

This success rate is 8% lower than the overall average for everyone else. England's left-footers have failed 50% of the time, compared to 30% for everyone else. Maybe more right-footers should shoot.

England fare best when shooting into the top half of the goal (83% success rate) but do so only 34% of the time. During the 66% of the time when they shoot low they score only 61% of the time, that is 22% worse than shooting high. Surely they should practise shooting high and in the real thing they should shoot there every single time.

Call me cynical or unappreciative of the pressures involved, but for tens of thousands of pounds a week, I would hope, no expect, that every single player in the squad could hit the top-right and top-left of the goal from 12 yards. Every single time. With a blindfold on. Seriously.

PART 4:
THE PLAYERS

"If you can't pass a ball properly, a bowl of pasta's not going to make that much difference."

– Harry Redknapp

"If your players are better than your opponents, 90 per cent of the time you will win." So said Johan Cruyff. The great players make the game seem easy even when they're talking about it. The problem for most football managers around the world these days is that a few clubs have much more money to get the best players and so it's a battle from the beginning to even be on that mythical 'level playing field'.

The table below illustrates how difficult this is proving to be in the Premiership. During the 2010/11 season the combined wage bill for the 20 clubs was reported to be a staggering £1.6bn. The majority of this was spent by just the top six sides:

	League position	Wage bill (£m)	% of total
Chelsea	2nd	191	11.9%
Manchester City	3rd	174	10.9%
Manchester United	1st	153	9.6%
Liverpool	6th	135	8.4%
Arsenal	4th	124	7.8%
Tottenham	5th	91	5.7%

All things being equal, each club would spend 5% of the total but there's no way that say, Swansea, could afford or be willing to shell out £80m per season on wages (their wage bill was around £17m when they won promotion in 2011). As it was the top six spenders accounted for 54.3% of the total wage bill leaving the other 45.7% spread between 14 other clubs.

The Summer Shopping Spree

Long gone are the days when a manager could solve an immediate problem by going out and buying (or selling) someone whenever he needed to. With only two transfer windows (the summer shopping spree and the January sales) open for top flight clubs to do their business, these two periods are seen to be increasingly important, by fans and commentators alike, in their club's fortunes. The transfer windows also put extra pressure on managers because prices can inflate as the clock ticks down and more gambles are taken. But how important are these windows, and does a flashing of the cheque book ensure an improved season?

I decided to start by looking at Europe's biggest spenders during the summer of 2009 to see how their spending has affected their on-field performance during 2009/2010. I wanted to see if higher spending really had the desired effect and, if so, demonstrate how much you would need to spend to improve your club's performance by a single point in the final league table. Firstly, these were the biggest spenders in Europe:

Rank	Team	League	Spending
1	Real Madrid	La Liga	£143.5m
2	Manchester City	Premiership	£98.0m
3	Barcelona	La Liga	£74.8m
4	Bayern Munich	Bundesliga	£53.4m
5	Napoli	Serie A	£43.8m
6	Juventus	Serie A	£36.6m
7	Fenerbahce	Super Lig	£24.3m
8	Aston Villa	Premiership	£24.1m
9	Hamburg	Bundesliga	£20.7m
10	Besiktas	Super Lig	£20.7m
11	Sevilla	La Liga	£19.7m
12	Benfica	Primeira Liga	£19.5m
13	Birmingham City	Premiership*	£17.6m
14	Bordeaux	Ligue 1	£16.6m
15	Lyon	Ligue 1	£16.4m
16	Wolverhampton W	Premiership*	£15.8m
17	Stoke City	Premiership	£15.3m
18	Galatasaray	Super Lig	£15.2m
19	Chelsea	Premiership	£14.5m
20	Wolfsburg	Bundesliga	£14.2m

* = newly promoted from the Championship

Obviously there are some surprises in the list. No Manchester United or Liverpool and were Birmingham City really the 13th biggest spenders in the whole of Europe? Did these clubs get value for money?

The biggest of the big spenders on our list, Real Madrid, finished with 78 points at the end of the 2008/09 season and ended 2009/10 season with 96 points, an improvement of 18 points, which means they spent £8m per point of improvement! Florentino Perez, the president of Real Madrid, might be justified in saying it was money well spent if they were to finish top, but his problem is Barcelona, who with 99 points retained the Spanish championship ahead of their great rivals. Barca's improvement from the last year was 12 points, a £6.5m per point ratio, which has allowed them to spend £60m less than Madrid and still keep ahead of them.

Of the 20 top spenders listed above, only 11 clubs actually ended the following season with more points than before. The two clubs promoted into the English Premiership both survived, meaning their investment was worth it. Benfica made no change and out of the six clubs to have actually got worse, there were some big losers. Juventus and Wolfsburg both finished 19 points worse off and Bordeaux dropped by 16 points. The clubs to make an improvement were as follows:

Rank	Club	League	Dif. Pts	Cost per Pt
1	Real Madrid	La Liga	+18	£8m
2	Man. City	Premiership	+17	£5.8m
3	Napoli	Serie A	+13	£3.4m
4	Fenerbahce	Super Lig	+13	£1.9m
5	Galatasaray	Super Lig	+3	£5.1m
6	B. Munich	Bundesliga	+3	£17.8m
7	Barcelona	La Liga	+9	£8.3m
8	Stoke City	Premiership	+2	£7.2m
9	Aston Villa	Premiership	+2	£12.1m
10	Chelsea	Premiership	+3	£4.8m
11	Lyon	Ligue 1	+1	£16.4m

The European Cup Winners' Cup was discontinued in 1999 and the Uefa (nee Fairs) Cup has undergone numerous tweaks, which has left us with the much-maligned Europa League, populated by Champions League cast-offs.

Was it all worth it? Manchester City, for all of their £98m, were still not guaranteed a Champions League place. Real Madrid, for their £143m, still couldn't capture La Liga. The message might be an old one but it's still relevant: spending money alone doesn't guarantee success, it needs to be spent wisely. If you're still not sure, just ask the bank managers of Juventus and Wolfsburg.

The main reason for the spending is not only to try and win one's domestic league, but to qualify for the holy grail of the Champions League. This competition has taken on such overriding importance that other European tournaments are seen as very much second-rate. So does spending, once you've qualified for the Champions League, help you progress?

Club	Amount Spent	Round reached
Chelsea	138.5m	Semi-finals
Manchester United	42.9m	Last 16
Real Madrid	35.0m	Quarter-finals
Juventus	30.5m	Last 16
Olympique Lyonnais	16.7m	Quarter-finals
FC Porto	10.0m	Winners
AC Milan	8.5m	Quarter-finals
Bayern Munich	4.0m	Last 16
AS Monaco	3.2m	Finalists
Deportivo La Coruna	2.5m	Semi-finals
VFB Stuttgart	2.2m	Last 16

[Note all figures in Euros, spending during the summer of 2003 and rounds reached from the 2003/04 season]

The other five teams that reached the last 16 (Arsenal, Lokomotiv Moscow, Celta de Vigo, Real Sociedad and Sparta Prague) spent less than 1m Euros, although some minor signings with undisclosed fees are not included.

Data for Europe-wide spending isn't always readily available but a complete set for the 2003/04 season is shown above. It was the last year that a 'small' team reached the final, and more amazing because two 'small' teams managed to do so. Porto actually spent the sixth largest amount before the start of the season and were rewarded by winning the cup (especially by the 8.5m Euros they spent on Benni McCarthy, who was their leading Champions League scorer). It didn't hurt that they had Jose Mourinho as their manager either.

Fellow finalists Monaco took a more cautious route, spending just 3.2m Euros on Emmanuel Adebayor but shrewdly taking Fernando Morientes on loan from Real Madrid – he scored a third of their European goals and finished the campaign with a tournament-leading nine goals.

Chelsea spent by far the most money in Europe. It was their first season under Roman Abramovich and, despite being the biggest earners from the Champions League during the 2003/04 season, they only recouped 29m Euros from the competition. Porto won 13m Euros from the cup to give them an overall profit, a rare occurrence, but lost their manager to Chelsea and, with him, any chance of repeating their triumph the following season.

Why Peter Shilton Should Have Won 200 England Caps

Peter Shilton made 1,005 appearances in league football and won a record 125 England caps between 1970 and 1990. Perhaps he should have won closer to 200 caps. Shilton played under numerous England managers (Sir Alf Ramsey, Don Revie, Ron Greenwood and Sir Bobby Robson), but he was unlucky that during the late-1970s and early-1980s, Greenwood couldn't decide on the first choice England goalkeeper and used a kind of rotation system between Shilton and Liverpool's Ray Clemence.

Liverpool had been the dominant team of the 1970s, but as the decade wound down, Shilton and his Nottingham Forest team knocked Liverpool from their perch, first beating them in the League Cup final and then taking the league championship before knocking the Merseysiders out of the European Cup on the way to winning it twice for themselves.

Despite the chopping and changing, Clemence was told he was first choice. "It was explained to me that I was number one unless I made some horrendous mistakes," said Clemence. But by late 1981 it was Shilton in goal as England qualified for the World Cup in Spain. Greenwood seemed to have changed his mind again, and when the

World Cup shirts were handed out Clemence was given the number one but then Shilton played every game in the tournament.

The pair's club records in the five years leading up to 1982 are remarkably similar:

	Shilton	*Clemence*
League games	203	204
Conceded	174	158
GAA	.857	.775
Clean sheets	93	96
Major trophies	5	5

GAA = Goals against average

Only when looking at the England performance of the two from the era when both Clemence and Shilton played can you separate them. It's clear that Shilton kept a higher proportion of clean sheets (13% more) and conceded fewer goals per game (0.32 goals per game less). Perhaps Shilton was 'punished' for his mistake which allowed Poland to knock England out of the 1974 World Cup at Wembley, but that mistake was a rarity and maybe England would have qualified for Argentina in 1978 had Shilton been used, just as he was reaching his peak with Forest.

Peter Shilton's England stats within the Clemence era:

	Pld	W	L	D	Win Pct	Gls	GAA	CS	CS%
W Cup qual.	6	3	1	2	66.7	4	0.67	3	50.0
W Cup finals	5	3	0	2	80.0	1	0.20	4	80.0
Euro qual.	10	6	1	3	75.0	5	0.50	6	60.0
Euro finals	1	0	1	0	0	1	1.00	0	0
Comp totals	22	12	3	7	70.5	11	0.50	13	59.1

Ray Clemence in the same period:

	Pld	W	L	D	Win Pct	Gls	GAA	CS	CS%
W Cup qual.	12	7	4	1	62.5	13	1.08	4	33.0
W Cup finals	0	0	0	0	0	0	0	0	0
Euro qual.	14	10	1	3	82.1	8	0.57	9	64.3
Euro finals	2	1	0	1	75.0	2	1.00	0	0
Comp totals	28	18	5	5	73.2	23	0.82	13	46.4

Bobby Moore: Over-Rated?

Jules Rimet gleaming in the summer sun. Bobby Moore carried high by his team-mates. But everyone knows the image, it's *the* iconic picture of English football. Moore himself has become an icon, partly because of that day, partly because of his many years of service to West Ham, Fulham and England, partly because of the tragedy of his untimely death at the age of 51. He has a statue at Wembley and Pele called him the fairest defender that he ever faced. But was he *that* good? He wasn't lightning quick, nor was he dominant in the air.

So what can be done to analyse Moore's quality? Like all pre-Premiership data, there is little to dissect his play and, though some video footage exists, it's too limited to fully investigate his whole career. What can be done though is to look at the effect his presence had on the results of his teams.

Moore made his England debut during the 1961/62 season and ended his international career after England failed to qualify for the 1974 World Cup. In between he played in 108 of England's 135 games. For all of his defensive qualities, Moore contributed little to England's goalscoring record, so it's the overall and defensive numbers that need to be crunched. How many games did

England win, how many clean sheets did they keep and how many goals, on average, did they concede?

England's record from 1961/62 to 1973/74 is as follows:

Measure	With Moore	Without Moore
Played	108	27
Won	67	13
Lost	18	3
Drawn	23	11
Goals for	213	50
Goals against	101	18
Win Pct	.727	.722
Clean sheet %	40.7%	48.2%
GAA	0.94	0.67

Before compiling these numbers I had a hunch that Moore's effect on the England team would have been only slightly beneficial. Not as great as some had heralded, but a positive effect none the less. I thought that England would have been a little bit better when he played. The figures in the table above don't agree with my expectations.

England weren't better when Moore played, they weren't even the same with or without him (which in itself would have been a severe knock on his reputation as a sterling defender). England overall were actually pretty much the same with or without Bobby Moore in the team (virtually identical winning percentages in each case), but defensively they were significantly worse when he played. With Moore in the team England were approximately 15% less likely to gain a clean sheet and conceded approximately 40% more goals. These aren't small differences and the 27 games without Moore are more than enough to iron out any fluke results.

It's a shame that there are no passing or assists statistics from the period because his influence there might have been substantial. It seems that the England icon's reputation has been built more on his qualities as a man and a leader than those as a world-class defender, which of course is no bad thing.

At the risk of being hung for treason, I thought I'd look at Moore's central defensive partner, Jack Charlton, as well. Charlton made his England debut in 1965 during the build-up to the World Cup and had an immediate impact. When you consider his effect on the team's defensive performance compared to Moore's it's quite startling.

Measure	With Charlton	Without Charlton
Win Pct	.833	.571
Clean sheet %	66.7%	28.6%
GAA	0.42	0.86

As can bee seen in the table above, Charlton improved England's Win Pct by a massive 26.2% (Moore improved it by only 0.5%). The side also kept twice as many clean sheets when he was in the side and conceded only half as many goals. Maybe it's time for another statue outside Wembley?

Why Dixie Dean Will Never Be Beaten

They are paid more than any other position, they are coveted the most, they are subject to the most devotion among fans. The goalscorer has always been the most important position on the pitch. You might control possession, might have a stone-wall defence, but if you can't score goals you won't win games.

When listing the game's greatest players it's hard not to list a disproportionate amount of goalscorers, as naturally they stay in the mind and take the glory. Recent seasons have seen the goalscoring race in La Liga between Cristiano Ronaldo and Lionel Messi reported around the world. The top goalscorer in the World Cup gets the Golden Boot. The numbers of league goals scored elevate the status of a striker to different levels. A scorer of 20 goals is hero worshipped, a scorer of 30 goals is a god.

So how would the nation's press react if someone popped up and scored 60 goals? It has happened just once in top flight history, and that was over 80 years ago. William 'Dixie' Dean of Everton completed the feat and no one has come close since. As usual it's hard to put the achievement into the context of today's game, but I'll try.

Dean played in the era of a 42-game season, so first I adjusted his tally to match up with the 38-game Premiership schedule. At the same rate he would have scored 54 goals in 38 matches. He also played in an era when goals were more plentiful. The 1927/28 season saw an average of 3.64 goals per game scored (compared to 2.81 in the 2011/12 Premiership campaign). You'd be forgiven for thinking that goals were easy to get back then and to an extent they were but no one came close to getting 60 like Dean. In fact he's also third on the all-time list with the 44 he scored four seasons later.

In order to get a feel of how he compares I divided the adjusted goal total of 54 by that season's GPG (3.64) to get a ratio of 14.8. This figure doesn't really mean anything other than to give a measure of the total goals in context with the difficulty of scoring them. I did the same calculation for Robin van Persie's 30 goals for Arsenal in 2011/12 and got a ratio of 10.7. Simply put this means that taking into account the difficulty of scoring, Dean's output was almost 40% better than van Persie's.

Below I've listed the adjusted goal totals and ratios for the 12 single-season highest top flight goalscorers in history and then, for comparison, a similar table for the top six Premiership era scorers.

Player	Team	Season	Gls	Adj to 38	Season GPG	Ratio
Dean	Everton	1927/28	60	54	3.64	14.8
Waring	Aston Villa	1930/31	49	44	3.69	11.9
Dean	Everton	1931/32	44	40	3.60	11.1
Halliday	Sunderland	1928/29	43	39	3.56	10.9
Harper	Blackburn	1925/26	43	39	3.45	11.3

Drake	Arsenal	1934/35	42	38	3.31	11.5
Watson	West Ham	1929/30	41	37	3.69	10.0
Greaves	Chelsea	1960/61	41	37	3.44	10.8
Richardson	West Brom.	1935/36	39	35	3.32	10.5
Charles	Leeds Utd	1956/57	38	34	3.38	10.1
Freeman	Everton	1908/09	38	38	3.11	12.2
Smith	Bolton	1920/21	38	34	2.50	13.6

38-game Premiership era:

Player	Team	Season	Gls	Adj to 38	Season GPG	Ratio
Cole	Newcastle	1993/94	34	31	2.59	11.9
Shearer	Blackburn	1995/96	31	31	2.60	11.9
Ronaldo	Man. Utd	2007/08	31	31	2.62	11.8
Henry	Arsenal	2003/04	30	30	2.66	11.3
Phillips	Sunderland	1999/00	30	30	2.79	10.8
Van Persie	Arsenal	2011/12	30	30	2.81	10.7

A list of the highest scoring top flight clubs in history:

Team	Season	GPG
Sunderland	1891/92	3.58
Blackburn Rovers	1889/90	3.55
Preston North End	1888/89	3.36
Sunderland	1892/93	3.33
Aston Villa	1930/31	3.05
Everton	1893/94	3.00
Arsenal	1932/33	2.81
Everton	1931/32	2.76
Arsenal	1934/35	2.74
Tottenham Hotspur	1960/61	2.74
Aston Villa	1894/95	2.73
Chelsea	2009/10	2.71
Tottenham Hotspur	1962/63	2.64
Wolverhampton Wanderers	1958/59	2.62
Aston Villa	1895/96	2.60
Sunderland	1935/36	2.60

Having looked at the domestic scoring records, I had to investigate the international ones. Who is the great international scorer of all time? Everything is more difficult at international level and the top international scorers of all time had to be very special players.

As usual, I only wanted to include competitive games and as there were very few pre-war qualifiers or tournament games I decided to keep my search to post-war players. I decided to split my lists into European and South American players. Other confederations have excellent goalscorers, but despite, for example Iran's Ali Daei netting 109 times, I have decided that the vast majority of his opponents were too weak to be compared with the rest. Maybe one day if I have a spare afternoon I'll do the calculations for all the other confederations.

I also chose a cut-off point for players to have to have scored 30 competitive international goals for consideration. This mean that Jimmy Greaves, for example, would not be included (he had only four goals in World Cup and European Championship games).

I was finalising the list during Euro 2012 and noted that two of the world's current stars, Messi and Ronaldo, would be absent. Messi, despite his white-hot club form for Barcelona, has a relatively poor international strike rate. At just 24 years old he has time on his side, but at 24 Pele had 15 goals in 13 games and Bobby Charlton had five goals in four games before blossoming later. Messi has nine in 43 for a strike rate of only 0.209 GPG.

Ronaldo on the other hand is 27 years old and had 30 competitive goals for Portugal in 64 games. As I watched the tournament I thought he would come up just short of the 30 goals required for inclusion. He uncharacteristically managed to miss two one-on-ones versus Denmark and was frustrated against Germany. Then he netted twice against Holland and again to beat the Czech Republic and I had to reach for my calculator.

Name	Nation	Pld	Gls	GPG
Gerd Muller	West Germany	31	39	1.258
Davor Suker	Croatia	43	32	0.744
David Villa	Spain	45	33	0.733
Karl-Heinz Rummenigge	West Germany	50	32	0.680
Miroslav Klose	Germany	65	42	0.646
Jan Koller	Czech Republic	53	33	0.623
Thierry Henry	France	51	30	0.588
Cristiano Ronaldo	Portugal	64	30	0.577
Toni Polster	Austria	55	31	0.564
Jurgen Klinsmann	Germany	57	30	0.526
Jon Dahl Tomasson	Denmark	62	32	0.516
Hakan Sukur	Turkey	76	39	0.513
Robbie Keane	Ireland	69	33	0.478
Raul	Spain	67	33	0.493

The table shows that only one European in history can claim more than a goal a game in competitive matches, 'Der Bomber', Gerd Muller, is well ahead, Davor Suker is second and Spain's David Villa in third is the highest ranked active player. Four Germans help make up the top ten, covering the 1970s, 1980s, 1990s and 21st century, helping to explain why they have been so formidable for so long. There are no Italians or Dutch in the list. Italy have had short-term goal machines such as Paolo Rossi and Salvatore Schillaci but no one over 30 goals.

Due to the fewer number of games played by South American nations, I lowered the threshold to 20 goals to determine that continent's all-time greatest scorer. Even at that level it eliminated such greats as the Brazilian Tostao (13 goals in 13 games) and Maradona (15 goals in 41 games, but his GPG of 0.366 was low anyway). Only seven players make the list and five are from Brazil. Like Germany, the great strikers cover a range of decades, this time back as far as Pele in the late 1950s.

Name	Nation	Pld	Gls	GPG
Pele	Brazil	26	26	1.000
Romario	Brazil	29	23	0.793
Ronaldo	Brazil	47	35	0.745
Gabriel Batistuta	Argentina	47	34	0.723
Bebeto	Brazil	33	20	0.606
Hernan Crespo	Argentina	43	26	0.605
Rivaldo	Brazil	38	22	0.579

The Greatest Player Of All Time

One of the great debates of any sport is who is the greatest player of all time? Different people will have different criteria that have to be met and different opinions on who it should be. As with most of this book, I'm less interested in opinions and more in facts. As usual I'll be looking at the increase in Win Pct as a fair way of seeing a player's impact on his team. It doesn't really matter when the player played, if he improves his team, while playing at the highest level, by the biggest amount then he has a good shout at being the greatest. This also meant that I could compare forwards and defenders on an equal footing.

My criteria were that the comparison had to be at the highest international level, this was all about the best of the best. There were some notable omissions. Messi and Ronaldo are still playing, so I'll consider them when they retire. Ferenc Puskas, Alfredo Di Stefano and George Best didn't play enough competitive games for a fair comparison, and while it would probably be widely agreed that they are top ten material, none is really considered the absolute best. Marco Van Basten isn't the greatest Dutch player of all time, and though he was a striker he didn't make the list of greatest goalscorers so there is little chance of being the greatest player.

Like anyone else, I had some preconceived ideas about who was the best. I'd grown up being told that Pele was the greatest, though I'd seen little of him myself. What I had seen was puzzling for a child. If he was the greatest, why did they always show him failing to score? Trying, but missing, from the halfway line. Being thwarted by Gordon Banks. Dummying a Uruguayan goalkeeper but then missing the open goal. I had seen a lot of Diego Maradona play though and was swept along with the tide of 'experts' saying he was the best of all. My personal favourite though, was Johan Cruyff. I was intrigued to see what I would find.

I worked out the Win Pct for each player's country during their international careers and analysed the improvement in the teams' results when each player appeared. I got quite a surprise:

		With				Without		
	P	W-D-L	GLS	Win Pct	P	W-D-L	Win Pct	Increase
Pele	26	22-3-1	26	.942	24	12-3-9	.563	.379
Cruyff	33	22-7-4	25	.772	11	4-1-6	.409	.363
Zidane	49	34-13-2	21	.827	21	6-12-3	.571	.256
Platini	41	23-7-11	15	.660	15	5-7-3	.567	.093
Eusebio	38	17-8-13	26	.553	3	1-1-1	.500	.053
Beckenbauer	47	31-14-2	5	.809	5	3-2-0	.800	.009
Charlton	29	18-4-7	14	.689	8	3-5-0	.688	-
Maradona	41	21-9-11	18	.622	18	8-9-1	.694	-(.072)

"Maradona will always be the greatest," said Eric Cantona. *"The crucial difference is that Maradona wasn't surrounded by great players; he had to carry the team. If you took Maradona out of Argentina they would not win the World Cup. Brazil without Pele would still have won."*

Everyone is entitled to an opinion, but with the information shown above I have to disagree with Mr Cantona most heartily. Pele is actually clear at the top of this very illustrious list. The assumption that Brazil were a great team without Pele is clearly wrong. They had some great players, but there was obviously something missing when Pele didn't take to the field as losing nine out of 24 games clearly shows.

The claim that they would win without him was tested when he all but missed the 1966 World Cup and they failed to win it for the only time between 1958 and 1970 (though they did manage to win the 1962 final without him). Amazingly, Brazil lost only one competitive game when Pele played and he scored 26 goals in those 26 games.

Not too far behind Pele is Cruyff. He raised Holland to great heights but failed to win a major tournament. Maradona still isn't on the list as we travel down past Zidane, Platini, Eusebio, Beckenbauer and Charlton. He actually comes eighth out of eight and is the only player on the list who has a negative impact on his team's Win Pct.

The comment that Argentina were average without him is another fallacy. They only lost once in 18 competitive games without their number ten, but lost 11 out of 41 when he played. And they won the 1978 World Cup without him, just as he was breaking on to the scene (having made his international debut in 1977). He undoubtedly had a great impact in 1986, but fell short in 1982, 1990 and 1994, whereas Pele won three World Cups. These trophies along with the stats above make it clear that the question of the greatest of all-time has been decisively answered. For now.

Interlude

Can You See It Coming?

It's always seemed to me that other countries take their national youth sides much more seriously than we do in England. I couldn't remember the last time that England had a decent showing at the World Youth Cup, so I had to look it up. It was a fourth place in 1981. I recognised a few of the names in the squad: Neil Webb, Paul Allen, Kevin Gage and Stewart Robson, but most were a mystery to me. Only Neil Webb went on to play any number of full internationals. The 1981 side lost in the semi-final to Qatar. Other nations seem to be able to translate their youth success into the senior side as the table below shows.

Medallists from World Youth Cups 1977 to 2009:

Senior World Cup	Year	Winners	Runners-up
	1977	USSR	Mexico
	1979	Argentina	USSR
	1981	W. Germany*	Qatar
1982 W. Germany*	1983	Brazil	Argentina
	1985	Brazil	Spain
1986 Argentina	1987	Yugoslavia	W. Germany
	1989	Portugal	Nigeria
1990 W. Germany			
	1991	Portugal	Brazil
	1993	Brazil*	Ghana
1994 Brazil*			
	1995	Argentina	Brazil
	1997	Argentina	Uruguay
1998 France			
	1999	Spain*	Japan
	2001	Argentina	Ghana
2002 Brazil			
	2003	Brazil	Spain*
	2005	Argentina	Nigeria
2006 Italy			
	2007	Argentina	Czech Rep.
	2009	Ghana	Brazil
2010 Spain*			

PART 5:
THE CHAMPIONS LEAGUE

"When you score one goal more than the other team in a cup tie it is always enough."

– Cesare Maldini

For a long time the premier club competition in Europe was called the European Champion Clubs' Cup, or European Cup for short. From 1955, each year each Uefa member nation could enter the winner of their domestic league, along with the current holders to play an unseeded straight knockout competition. Each round until the final was played over two legs before the showpiece event on a usually neutral ground. It was a difficult competition to enter, never mind win. The absence of any group phases meant that even a single defeat could be fatal.

In the 1990s Uefa decided to rebrand and expand the competition. The Champions League was born and has had several formats over the past two decades. The number of annual entries now approaches 80 clubs, with the top performing nations able to put four teams into the draw. It isn't really a league, and it isn't only competed for by champions, but there you go.

Despite being banned after the Heysel Stadium disaster, English clubs have historically done very well in European competition, but which is the most dominant? With the extra games to play, how many players do you really need and is it really that different to the early days? How important is it to play the second leg at home? What effect does a European tie have on your league form? How have imported players affected the competition? Is it fair to let losing Champions League teams into the Europa League and how would the list of Champions League winners really look if only the champions of their own country were allowed to compete? The Champions League anthem is playing, you know the one, so let's get started.

The 21st Century Squad System – Is It Really That Different To Real Madrid In The 1950s?

Many things have changed in the game of football today from the quaint old days of the maximum wage, all-British squads of players and the 2-3-5 formation. But some things that we think have changed really haven't.

These days, many column inches are filled with discussions about the merits of the squad-rotation systems employed by some managers, and the large number of first team players that fill the ranks of certain clubs. One side of the argument puts these points forward as further examples of the ills of the modern game: foreign managers that like to tinker too much and big clubs that sign too many players and let them go stale in the reserves. But are these really new phenomena? For this example I decided to look at the squads used in the Champions League/ European Cup over the years. Here's how it panned out.

Manchester United have been Champions League perennials in the last few years, and their squad is thought to have as much, if not more, depth than any English side. Here's how many players they've used in Europe during five recent seasons:

Season	Stage Reached	Games	Players	Ever-present
2008-09	Finalists	13	23	0
2007-08	Winners	13	24	0
2006-07	Semi-finalists	12	19	3
2005-06	First group	8	17	4
2004-05	Last 16	10	25	0
Totals	–	56	108	7

Compared to the old European Cup format, today's teams need to play around twice as many games to win the 'cup with the big ears', and you'd expect current teams to use more players. From the above table, United's player usage, for an average of 12 games, would see them use 22 players. But what about the old-time teams?

For comparison, I decided to go back to the earliest five years of the European Cup (a decision also made necessary because until the non-champions of each country were admitted into the competition it was pretty much unheard of for a team to play in the cup five years in a row; Real Madrid managed this feat between 1955 and 1960 because they won the cup for the first five years of its existence). Did teams really use the same players over and over? Especially back in the days when there were no substitutions allowed.

Season	Stage Reached	Games	Players	Ever-present
1959-60	Winners	7	18	6
1958-59	Winners	7	18	6
1957-58	Winners	7	18	4
1956-57	Winners	8	16	1
1955-56	Winners	7	19	3
Totals	–	36	89	20

Real Madrid obviously weren't surviving on 13 or 14 man squads. In fact, over the five-year period, they had a player usage of approximately 28% more than the number used by United half a century later. If they had used their squad in the same way during today's Champions League, it would equate to a usage of 32 players over a 13-game campaign, a considerable amount more than the Manchester United of today.

They had a more settled core of their side (shown in the number of players ever-present in their European campaigns), which perhaps helped them to their five successive wins. Legendary striker Alfredo di Stefano played in all of their games in four of the five seasons, while midfielder Zarraga and speedy winger Gento did so in three of the campaigns.

It was skilful management that allowed Madrid to stay at the top of the European game, while slowly tweaking the squad and replacing aging players when necessary. By the 1960 final there were seven changes to the team that played in the 1956 final. They arguably saved their best until last, as they beat Eintracht Frankfurt 7-3 at Hampden Park – it could have been ten. The combination of clever leadership and supreme skill on the pitch means that their five-year reign is unlikely ever to be beaten.

Home Leg Advantage

Many cup competitions around the world use the two-leg system whereby each side plays once at home and the team with the higher aggregate score goes through. This has often caused debate over which leg it is preferable to have at home. Some might say that getting a good first leg lead is most advantageous, while others argue that a second leg at home is more important because you know exactly how you need to approach the game and what is required for qualification. I looked back over 100 recent European knockout ties in the Champions and Europa Leagues, for ease of calculations if nothing else, and noted how the home side did in each leg and how that related to their progression. Here's what I found:

First Leg at Home

	Home team	Qualify	%
Wins	45	33-12	73%
Draws	30	10-20	33%
Losses	25	1-24	4%

The team with the first leg at home has a Win Pct of .600 and winning the first game is vital to stay in the competition. A home win helped put 73% of sides through while a home draw meant that two out of three of all teams were ultimately eliminated. A home loss in the first leg basically spells the end.

Second Leg at Home

	Home team	Qualify	%
Wins	56	45-11	80%
Draws	24	12-12	50%
Losses	20	2-18	10%

The team playing the second leg at home has a Win Pct of .680. This figure, higher than the first leg home teams, indicates that the home side is more likely to go for a win, often because they have no choice. Winning the second leg at home is more decisive than the first leg as 80% of teams then progress (compared to 73%) and a home loss is slightly more likely to allow qualification. However, if you lose either leg the chance of going through is down to a measly 7%.

Hung Over – What Effect Does a Midweek European Game Have On Your Weekend?

With today's super-fit squads, pampered players and charter flights, you could be forgiven for thinking that a midweek game would have little or no effect on a team's results the next weekend. But you'd be wrong. Whichever way you look at it, English sides perform worse after a midweek Champions League game than they would otherwise.

The four English sides that played most often in Europe recently (Manchester United, Arsenal, Liverpool and Chelsea) had a combined winning percentage of 71.6% after playing in Europe, compared to a combined percentage of 78.7% when they didn't. The drop of 7.1% equates to a three or four-point difference in their final points total, suggesting that if they weren't in the Champions League the big four would stretch even further ahead from the rest of the pack.

I initially looked into this effect several years ago and found that clubs performed worse after an away trip, which is perhaps understandable though not really excusable.

But, interestingly, the drop in form is even more marked after they play a Champions League game at home. Here are the Win Pcts from the 2008/09 season:

Team	No Euro	Away Euro	Home Euro	All Euro
Arsenal	.589	.917	.667	.792
Chelsea	.786	.800	.600	.700
Liverpool	.846	.583	.833	.708
Man. United	.875	.800	.500	.650
Totals	.787	.772	.659	.716

A couple of things come to mind when looking at these numbers. Liverpool eventually finished only four points behind Manchester United in the Premiership title race, but if they hadn't performed so badly after an away European trip (just .583) they would have had a real chance of winning their first title in nearly 20 years. The other number that sprung out was Arsenal's .917 after a European away trip. However, the games they played to gain that high percentage were all against teams towards the bottom of the league, two of which went on to be relegated. Arsenal's form after home European games was much more in keeping with the rest of their season. I was a little surprised by these figures and so had a quick look at the previous season (2007/08) where Liverpool also struggled after away games (.500) and Arsenal did better (.800 compared to 0.67) after an away game.

I followed it up for the 2009/10 season, with Arsenal pushing for the title and Liverpool struggling to get fourth spot. The numbers were as follows:

Team	No Euro	Away Euro	Home Euro	All Euro
Arsenal	.725	.900	.500	.722
Chelsea	.738	.750	.833	.786
Liverpool	.650	.625	.375	.500
Man. United	.864	.250	.500	.358
Totals	.753	.647	.536	.597

[Note on these tables: European games between English sides are not included, Liverpool's 2009/10 results include their Champions League and Europa League games.]

So the trend continued with the four sides' combined Win Pct dropping from .753 to .597 after a European tie. Arsenal continued to buck this trend after away European games (.900 – but again they played most of these games against sides from the foot of the Premiership), while Manchester United would have had a clear lead in the Premiership if it were not for their poor post-European results. If you liked a flutter (which of course, is not something I recommend) it might have been good to bet on United losing after an away European game, as their winning percentage in those situations was down to a relegation-like .250.

Bringing it up to date I found the following for 2011/12:

Team	No Euro	Away Euro	Home Euro	All Euro
Arsenal	.633	.750	.625	.688
Chelsea	.558	1.000	.417	.708
Man. City	.839	.700	.700	.700
Man. United	.786	.800	.900	.850
Totals	.705	.825	.650	.738

As had already been seen, the effect of playing in Europe is more pronounced for some teams than for others. While it doesn't affect everyone to the same degree, the ones that handle it best generally do better. Manchester City performed 13% worse after a European game but it was just enough to see off Manchester United for the title, even though United got a slight boost. Arsenal continued to confound by playing better after an away European game, 12% better in fact, and it wasn't because they had any easier games. Their three wins came against Stoke, Everton and Spurs.

One of the big stories of the season was that of Chelsea. Changing managers part of the way through the campaign still didn't stop them from winning their first Champions League trophy. Along the way it had a strange impact on their league form. After a home game they slumped to an unimpressive .417 but after an away match they had a 100% record, winning six out of six. Perhaps a psychologist could explain it by the boost and excitement they got from their excellent away results carrying over, but why didn't it help the home form at all?

Imports Into The Champions League

The number of non-European players competing in Europe has risen dramatically since the 1990s and continues to do so. In 1990 there were 51, by 1998 it was 120, then 204 in 2006 and up to 250 in 2010.

Domestically there has always been an argument about the use of more imported players damaging the development of home grown talent, and people point, perhaps unfairly, to the performance of the national team as a symptom of this. It doesn't seem to be harming club sides though. For them it's simply a case of getting the best players no matter where they come from.

This is borne out in the performance of teams in the Champions League. Here's a table of how many teams have reached the last four during the last 12 years, showing how many teams did so from each country and how many nationalities play in that particular league:

	Teams	Nationalities
Portugal	1	4
Holland	1	6
France	2	9
Germany	5	16
Italy	7	15
Spain	15	15
England	17	34

It's fairly clear that the nations employing most nationalities are getting more teams deeper into the competition and as long as non-Europeans can be purchased relatively cheaply, it's a practice that is sure to rise in the future.

The Real Champions of the Champions League

If it really was the Champions League, only the reigning
champions of each country would be allowed to play in it.
Here is a list of the 'real' winners when the non-champions
have been removed:

1993 Marseille
1994 AC Milan
1995 Ajax
1996 Juventus
1997 Borussia Dortmund
1998 Real Madrid
1999 Manchester United, should have been a final
    between Juventus and Dynamo Kyiv
2000 Real Madrid, should have been a final between
    Bayern Munich and Barcelona
2001 Bayern Munich
2002 Real Madrid
2003 AC Milan, should be Juventus
2004 Porto
2005 Liverpool, should be AC Milan
2006 Barcelona
2007 AC Milan, should have been Chelsea
2008 Manchester United
2009 Barcelona, should be Manchester United
2010 Internazionale
2011 Barcelona
2012 Chelsea, should have been Barcelona

Second Class Citizens?

The Europa League has always been the most maligned of the European competitions. Starting as the Inter City Fairs Cup before being changed to the Uefa Cup, it was seen as a second class European alternative. The 'nearly teams' (finishing third, fourth, fifth in the domestic league) were being given something to play for, but when those nearly teams were allowed into the Champions League, the Uefa Cup became even more of a side-show, prompting Uefa to rebrand it as the Europa League.

Recently it's become even more soul-destroying for the teams battling through endless rounds of competition because the teams finishing third in their Champions League groups are now parachuted into the Europa League just as the knockout phases begin. The question is, do these 'losers' from the Champions League take it seriously? The answer is yes.

In the five seasons between 2007 and 2012, 40 Champions Leagues sides joined the Europa League in the last 32. Out of these 40, two have gone on to win it out of the five occasions. Here's how all the Champions League teams have gone on:

Round	Teams	% of that Round
Final	5	50%
Semi-finals	9	45%
Quarter-finals	7	18%
Last 16	12	15%
Last 32	40	25%

Eight Champions League teams per season join the round of 32, 25% of the total clubs, but by the final they take up 50% of the places.

National Domination Of The Club Competitions

Fans can be very protective of their own league, thinking it is superior to the others, but which league has produced the most winners of European silverware? I looked back through the finals of the Inter City Fairs Cup/Uefa Cup/Europa League, the European Cup Winners' Cup and the European Cup/Champions League and tabulated the winners by country and separated them by decade to see how the balance of power changed over the past 60 years.

1950s	1960s	1970s	1980s	1990s	2000s+
Spain 4	England 7	England 9	England 6	Italy 12	Spain 10
England 1	Spain 6	Germany 6	Spain 5	Germany 5	England 4
	Italy 6	Holland 4	Italy 4	Spain 4	Portugal 3
	Portugal 3	Belgium 3	Belgium 3	England 4	Italy 3
	Croatia 2	Italy 3	Sweden 2	France 2	Russia 2
	Germany 2		Holland 2		
			Germany 2		

The top five countries from each decade are noted. English clubs were banned from Europe between 1985 and 1990 before gradually being re-introduced. Clubs were arranged as being from the countries they are in now (e.g. Dinamo Zagreb in Croatia not Yugoslavia). England were the dominant team of the 1970s when the national side was poor, missing out on qualification for the 1974 World Cup, 1976 European Championship and 1978 World Cup. The English club teams that did so well used mainly British players, so how good would a GB team have been in those days?

Interlude: The Magic Of The Cups

The FA Cup – Still Romantic?

The 'romance' or the 'magic' of the FA Cup are phrases that are always uttered every January when the third round kicks off and the big teams join in. They show clips of famous upsets in the past, usually on muddy pitches, with commentators getting carried away. But does that magic exist anymore or has the money in the game crushed it out of existence? Since the Second World War I looked at 40 years of results and found that teams from the lower divisions did occasionally make it into the sixth round (the quarter-finals):

How many times from Fourth Division :	3	1%
From Third Division:	22	7%
From Second Division:	74	23%
From First Division:	221	69%

Then I looked at the past decade to see how that had changed:

How many times from League 2:	0	0%
From League 1:	2	3%
From the Championship:	13	16%
From the Premiership:	65	81%

Even though some Premiership sides are reported to not take it so seriously anymore, they are dominating the FA Cup more than ever. Sides from the fourth tier no longer get a sniff, those from the third tier have halved in number and the Championship sides get to the sixth round a third less. Looks like those old grainy clips will be shown for a few more years yet.

The League Cup – Does Anybody Care?

The League Cup has always been seen as the least important of the three major domestic competitions. With interest in the FA Cup falling away it seems natural that the League Cup would suffer too. Attendances are said to be falling and Premiership sides often put out reserve teams. However, on closer inspection, the top teams seem to be winning it more often than ever and crowds are on the way up, not down.

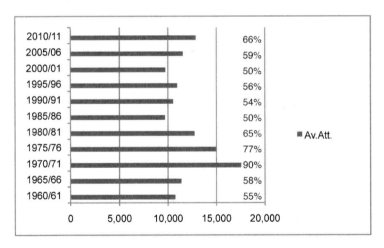

The highest ever average attendance, in 1971/72, was 19,489.

Taking snapshots of the average League Cup attendances every five years going back to its inception in the early 1960s you can see that attendances have generally been on the up for the past 30 years. As for the big sides not caring, how come they have taken 75% of the finals places over the past decade? Maybe their reserve sides are just so much better than everyone else's first team?

Club	Finals 2002 to 2012
Liverpool	4
Manchester United	4
Chelsea	3
Spurs	2
Arsenal	2

PART 6:
THE MANAGERS

"Before we won the championship, I told the lads exactly how many goals we would score and how many points. I was exactly right. I'm brilliant!"

– Malcolm Allison, 1972

"Any manager will tell you they'd rather win one and lose two than draw three because you get more points."

– Les Ferdinand

Giovanni Trapattoni says it's easy for a manager to make a team worse, but hard to make it better. Though he has less responsibilities than a generation ago, the manager still has to be a little bit of something different to lots of people. A friend, a teacher, a tough taskmaster, he has to know what works with who. He now has to analyse vast amounts of player data and liaise with nutritionists, video technicians and, God forbid, agents, to keep his team in with a chance.

Long gone are the days of sheepskin coats and deals being struck in the local café, it's all big business today, but the range and diversity of the top managers is still a joy to behold, and they give us lots to investigate. There might just be some good tips here for chairmen and CEOs too.

Is the Manager of the Month award really a curse? Is there an optimum length of employment for a manager? Do new managers instantly get a team to play better? Which England manager has really performed the best? How much of the success of the Brian Clough/Peter Taylor duo was down to the latter? Who has been the greatest domestic manager of all time? All this will be revealed, read on.

Manager Of The Month

Like any statistical analysis, there needs to be some context applied to the results of any survey and this is a prime example. For years I've read that winning the Manager of the Month award is a sure sign that your club is about to start losing. There are numerous examples of this being true, but is it a curse (of course there's no such thing) or is there some reasoning to clarify the numbers?

During each season there are nine monthly presentations running from August to April and to investigate what might be going on I called up a list of winners over a four-season span, from 2006/07 to 2009/10. I kept my data to that covering the Premiership because the hierarchy of managers was more obvious for the casual fan to recognise at first glance. Sir Alex Ferguson is a more established and successful manager than Gary Megson for example. I then went back and compiled a spreadsheet of each manager's performance during the month in which they won the award.

As you'd expect, this gave rise to a list of pretty high Win Pcts. The names on the list were also mostly as you'd predict: Wenger, Moyes, Ferguson, etc. Seventeen of the 36 winners had teams finishing in the top four and 28 of them finished in the top eight. There were a few surprises too: Coppell, Brown, Southgate, McLeish. This is where a fairly arbitrary line had to be drawn. Which were the 'good' managers who you would expect to win the award every now and then and which were the 'bad' managers who might win it once before their teams head back to the relegation zone?

'Good' and 'bad' isn't meant as a slight to any of the 'bad' managers. They have often performed miracles to get there in the first place, but in a ranking of Premiership teams the ones they manage are among the weakest. It's often these 'bad' managers that give rise to the curse myth.

Below is a table showing the combined records of the nine monthly winners for each of the four seasons. They are split into Win Pcts for when they won the award, the record of their team for the calendar month following the award and the record of their club during the other seven months of that season. How much better than average did they play during the award-winning month and how much worse did they play after it, if at all?

Year	Month of Award Pct				Following Month Pct				Rest of Season Pct			
	W	D	L		W	D	L		W	D	L	
06/07	31	4	2	.891	14	10	11	.543	74	43	44	.593
07/08	32	4	2	.895	13	13	9	.557	96	52	44	.635
08/09	29	4	2	.886	20	5	10	.643	62	53	71	.476
09/10	29	10	0	.872	10	10	13	.455	92	36	54	.604
Total	121	22	6	.886	57	38	43	.551	324	184	213	.577

At first glance the results seem quite startling with a massive Win Pct of .886 during the winning months and then an enormous fall of over 33% the following month. Closer inspection tells us more. Look at the overall figure for how the teams perform during the rest of the season, the Win Pct is .577. This means the clubs only perform about 2% worse in the month after the award than their average in that season. The award-winning month was actually way above the average, which is why the award was usually won in the first place.

I looked at a group of individual managers and searched for any more detailed effects. The obvious starting point was Sir Alex Ferguson. During the 36 months of my analysis he won the award seven times, way ahead of the next best winners (Martin O'Neill and David Moyes with four each. Moyes won each of his awards during the latter part of a season).

Ferguson won awards in August, September, October, January, February, March and April during these four seasons, winning all 28 matches during the seven months. In the seven individual months after each award his Win Pct dropped from 1.000 to .722, a fall of 28%. You wouldn't expect a team like Manchester United to drop very much at all during a season. They have a few ups and downs but 28% over seven months taken from four different seasons is huge. But look at the rest of their games. They averaged a Win Pct of .745, so the seven award-winning months were actually way ahead of their average and these bursts of excellence were what led them to a hat-trick of titles in this period.

If it can seem like a consistently high-performing club like Manchester United can suffer from the 'curse' it's no wonder that all the other clubs, when they have a good month but then drop back to normality, really seem to be cursed. There is no curse, it's just that most clubs perform abnormally well for short bursts of time.

The origin of the curse myth is easily seen when the likes of these managers were winners: Gareth Southgate .667 in August 2008 then .000 in September (Middlesbrough were eventually relegated). Sam Allardyce at Bolton went from .833 to .250, Roy Hodgson from .800 to .000 and Mark Hughes did exactly the same. A highly respected manager like Martin O'Neill might also have felt jinxed. Four straight wins in November 2007 were followed by five games without a single win. These are simply parts of the ebb and flow of a football fixture list. Apart from the very top and bottom of the division you'll get bursts of good and bad, irrespective of winning a monthly award.

Optimum Time Of Management?

"You're not a real manager unless you've been sacked," once quipped Malcolm Allison. It's something that virtually all managers expect at some time in their career, but some clubs seem to have a higher turnover than others, a practise that is unlikely to bring success. Looking at the list of managerial changes between 1980 and 2010 I listed the clubs which had had the most managers and which had had the least.

Most managers		Least	
Notts County	22	Man Utd	3
C Palace	21	Arsenal	5
Carlisle	21	Crewe	6
Swansea	20	Liverpool	7
QPR	20	Ipswich	8
Cardiff	20	Port Vale	8
		West Ham	8

The three most successful teams in that period fill three of the four clubs with least managers, while the list on the left is mainly filled with clubs that have spent many seasons in the lower reaches. Alex Ferguson was famously on the verge of being sacked at Manchester United in 1989. In hindsight, and 12 titles later, I think they're pretty glad that they didn't.

The Goods In The Back: Brian Clough and Peter Taylor

"I'm not equipped to manage successfully without Peter Taylor. I am the shop window and he is the goods in the back."

– Brian Clough

Brian Clough has become a mini-industry of his own in the last few years as the subject of numerous books, films, and documentaries. I was lucky enough to meet the man on several occasions and once had an hour-long interview with him. He was everything you'd expect him to be and more.

He and Peter Taylor had famously taken Derby County to unknown heights in the early 1970s before falling out with the board and ending up at Brighton & Hove Albion. Clough soon left for his ill-fated spell at Leeds while Taylor stayed on the south coast, just missing out on promotion in 1976. By then Clough had moved to Nottingham Forest and despite moving the City Ground side to eighth in the Second Division he wanted some help. "We had one meeting in Majorca," Clough told me. "It was a half-hour job, sitting in the sunshine. Then he went on with his holidays and I came back to work. It all started from that."

What started was probably the most amazing transformation of any club in history. In the first year back together they won promotion with Forest to the First Division. Then the following season they won the First Division title. Twelve months later they went and won the European Cup. Then they retained it. It's highly unlikely that such a feat will ever be repeated. Taylor retired in 1982 but within months was back managing Derby County. He and Clough fell out over a transfer and they never spoke again. Taylor died in 1990 and Clough passed away in 2004.

There are statues of Clough in Nottingham and Middlesbrough, where he played. Only outside Pride Park in Derby is there a statue of the two of them. Has Peter Taylor been unfairly written out of the history books? I broke down the records of Clough's managerial career by club to see what happened when he worked alone and the difference with Taylor.

Wins-draws-losses for Brian Clough and Peter Taylor, alone and together, by club:

	Clough	Clough+Taylor	Taylor	Trophies
Hartlepools United	1-0-0	34-13-31	-	-
Derby County	-	126-61-77	-	L
Leeds United	1-2-3	-	-	-
Brighton & HA	-	12-8-12	38-19-35	-
Nottingham Forest	20-20-19	121-74-57	-	L, 2LC, 2EC
Derby County	-	-	22-21-20	-
Nottingham Forest	190-114-144	-		2LC
Totals	212-136-166	293-156-177	60-40-55	
Win Pct	.545	.593	.516	

(L = league championship, LC = League Cup, EC = European Cup).

Together they won two league championships, two League Cups and two European Cups in 12 seasons split between Forest and Derby. In 15 season by themselves, Clough won two more League Cups and Taylor won nothing. Clough needed the spark of his relationship with Taylor to make him one of the greatest.

In league terms, Taylor alone only just managed to win more games than he lost (Win Pct .516) and these were games in the Second and Third Divisions. Clough's solo years were all in the top flight and he won .545, but together with Taylor in the top flight that figure rises to .613. Over a 42-game season this is equivalent to a rise of three more wins per season. That might not sound like a lot but it would have pushed Forest into the runners-up spot in 1982/83, made them champions in 1983/84, pushed them to third in 1986/87, runners-up again in 1987/88, third in 1989/90 and could have saved them from relegation in Clough's final season, 1992/93.

New Manager Syndrome

A team is on a losing run, it's at the bottom end of the table and pressure is mounting from the fans. The inevitable happens, the manager is sacked. Out comes the chairman or CEO with comments like "we needed a change of direction", "new ideas", "we have become stale, things need freshening up".

Is a mid-season change really worthwhile? Depending on the time of the sacking, the new manager might only be able to work with the same players who got the club into trouble in the first place. Can he give them an immediate boost or would it have been better to wait until the summer and let the new man start afresh? Everyone expects the players to try and prove their worth for the new man and go and win his first game in charge, and that usually happens, right?

Below is a table showing the mid-season Premiership changes from the past few seasons. I've shown the club's record in the last ten games under the old manager, what result they got in the first match under the new man and what their record was in the first ten games with him and the difference compared to the last ten games with the old guy.

Last 10	New Manager	Club	Season	First	First 10	Dif
.200	Terry Connor	Wolves	2011/12	drew	.200	0
.350	Martin O'Neill	Sunderland	2011/12	won	.750	.400
.200	Mark Hughes	QPR	2011/12	lost	.300	.100
.450	Alan Pardew	Newcastle	2010/11	won	.450	0
.450	Steve Kean	Blackburn	2010/11	lost	.350	-(.100)
.450	Kenny Dalglish	Liverpool	2010/11	lost	.700	.250
.250	Roy Hodgson	WBA	2010/11	drew	.650	.400
.250	Avram Grant	Portsmouth	2009/10	lost	.300	.050
.550	Robert Mancini	Manchester C.	2009/10	won	.700	.150
.400	Owen Coyle	Bolton	2009/10	lost	.400	0
.350	Brian Laws	Burnley	2009/10	lost	.150	-(.200)
.300	Iain Dowie	Hull City	2009/10	lost	.250	-(0.50)
.350	average				.433	.083

Of the 12 managers on the list, only three managed to win their first game in charge. The average initial improvement over the first ten games was just 8%. Four of the 12 were relegated anyway and only four managers managed more than a 10% improvement. When taking into account the massive pay-offs that some managers receive it might be better to stick with the man that was deemed the best for the job not long beforehand.

In most cases a team on the way down goes down. Most recently, Terry Connor had a torrid time at Wolves and they failed to win any of his 13 games in charge, finishing bottom of the table, 12 points adrift of safety. His record was equally as bad as the last ten games had been under Mick McCarthy. Mark Hughes did better, winning six of 17 games, but needing results to go their way on the final day in order to stay up.

In the previous season, Steve Kean failed to improve Blackburn at all (in fact they were 10% worse) and the following year they were relegated. The managerial merry-go-round saw Kenny Dalglish return to Liverpool where he replaced Roy Hodgson. Dalglish improved Liverpool by 25% while Hodgson went to West Bromwich Albion and improved them by 40%. A year later Dalglish was sacked and Hodgson was the England manager. Was the Liverpool board trigger happy?

The average Win Pct for a Premiership club to sack its manager is .350 so a good start is vital for some managers or they'll be looking for work again before Christmas.

The Toughest Job In Football? The England Managers

"I'm not saying we shouldn't have a foreign manager, but I think he should definitely be English."

– Paul Merson

The only true measure of a team's success is the number of games it wins. Not goal difference, not the attractiveness of a team's play as some purists would like to cling to, but the good old fashioned two, or rather three, points for a win. Playing nice football and/or scoring lots of goals along the way is a bonus, but it's the winning that matters. A fan walking home is more likely to be content with a poor 1-0 win than an entertaining 4-2 loss.

Other writers and newspapers have used friendlies in their analyses, but there are far too many variables to validate their usage. Teams often use friendlies to experiment with personnel or formation: at half-time we now see hatfuls of substitutions and star players with minor injuries are likely to be rested, and so on. It's the competitive games that really count and so it's by these that players and managers should be measured.

The only thing that might be put ahead of winning games is winning trophies but, as we are looking at England managers in this section, and England have only ever won one of these, it's not something that we can judge, so we'll stick to the percentages. To get the ball rolling, here are the winning percentages for all England managers in all games (friendlies, qualifiers and tournament games):

	Pld	W	D	L	F	A	Pts	Win Pct
Roy Hodgson	6	4	2	0	7	3	9	.833
Fabio Capello	42	28	8	6	89	35	64	.762
Alf Ramsey	113	69	27	17	112	98	165	.730
Sven-Goran Eriksson	67	40	17	10	128	61	97	.724
Terry Venables	23	12	9	2	35	13	33	.717
Glenn Hoddle	28	17	6	5	42	13	40	.714
Ron Greenwood	55	33	12	10	93	40	78	.709
Walter Winterbottom	139	78	33	28	383	196	189	.679
Bobby Robson	95	47	30	18	154	60	124	.653
Graham Taylor	38	18	13	7	62	32	49	.645
Joe Mercer	7	3	3	1	9	7	9	.643
Don Revie	29	14	8	7	49	25	36	.621
Steve McClaren	18	9	4	5	32	12	22	.611
Kevin Keegan	18	7	7	4	26	15	21	.583
Howard Wilkinson	2	0	1	1	0	2	1	.250
Stuart Pearce	1	0	0	1	2	3	0	.000
Peter Taylor	1	0	0	1	0	1	0	.000

It's tables like this that have been printed in recent years alongside articles about the new England manager (McClaren, Capello, Hodgson) to show that Alf Ramsey and Terry Venables are up there with the best and that Don Revie was a complete failure. I don't like tables like this, they are diluted by too much irrelevant information. Here instead is a table of performance in only competitive games:

Listed by tournament, with W-D-L:

	World Cup	Euros	Total	Win Pct
Fabio Capello	10-3-1	5-3-0	15-6-1	.818
Sven-Goran Eriksson	16-2-2	8-2-2	24-4-4	.750
Roy Hodgson	0	2-0-2	2-0-2	.750
Ron Greenwood	9-3-3	8-2-1	17-5-4	.750
Glenn Hoddle	8-1-3	0	8-1-3	.708
Don Revie	3-0-1	3-2-1	6-2-2	.700
Terry Venables	0	3-1-1	3-1-1	.700
Steve McClaren	0	7-2-3	7-2-3	.667
Bobby Robson	12-10-4	10-3-4	22-13-8	.663
Alf Ramsey	8-3-3	10-3-4	18-6-7	.656
Walter Winterbottom	16-5-7	0-1-0	16-6-7	.655
Graham Taylor	5-3-2	3-5-1	8-8-3	.632
Kevin Keegan	0-0-1	4-4-3	4-4-4	.500
Howard Wilkinson	0-1-0	0	0-1-0	.500

The first thing to note is that foreign managers have been the best. Unless Roy Hodgson can carry on unbeaten for any length of time they are likely to remain at the top of the table for some time.

Alf Ramsey won the World Cup. There isn't much more to say about him, but his overall Win Pct is worse than Don Revie's. Steve McClaren is ahead of Bobby Robson. The facts of how the team competed are too often swallowed up in the perception of the manager as a person. Graham Taylor made the mistake of allowing a camera crew to follow him around while McClaren will probably never use an umbrella again.

A perennial talking point for England fans is who should have got the England job in the past and what might have been. Brian Clough is often termed the greatest manager England never had, but can we predict what he might have achieved?

The following table illustrates the record of England managers in their role of domestic club manager for the five top flight years prior to their taking the England post:

Name	5yr %	England %	Change
Ron Greenwood	.462	.750	+28.8%
Roy Hodgson	.473	.750	+27.7%
Steve McClaren	.454	.667	+21.3%
Glenn Hoddle	.520	.708	+18.8
Terry Venables	.544	.700	+15.6
Alf Ramsey	.601	.656	+15.5
Graham Taylor	.517	.632	+11.5%
Fabio Capello	.723	.818	+9.5%
Sven-Goran Eriksson	.668	.750	+8.2%
Bobby Robson	.593	.663	+7%
Don Revie	.698	.700	+2%
Kevin Keegan	.656	.500	-15.6%

Howard Wilkinson only managed for one competitive game and has been discounted; Walter Winterbottom had no experience of managing prior to taking the England job.

So what does this information tell us? Well, ten of the 12 managers have a Win Pct of about .630 to .750 in their competitive games. The only managers (Keegan, .500 and

Capello, .818, and even Hodgson's .750) to be significantly away from this figure were in the job for only a relatively small number of games.

More telling, perhaps, is the difference in club management success that we can see between the managers. Of course it doesn't follow that a very successful club manager would automatically transfer that success to the international stage, but surely the better his club record the better chance he has of succeeding.

The above table raises the question: why do club managers with a domestic record of less than .500 get the 'biggest job in the country'? Greenwood, McClaren and Hoddle were all average at best. At least Greenwood (with the help of a particularly weak qualifying group for Europa 80: Northern Ireland were the second best side in the group and England beat them 4-0 and 5-1) managed to boost his Win Pct above that of an average manager. Some of the appointments were clearly influenced by the need to have an Englishman in the job. Now that barrier has been broken we have seen what is possible.

But when Greenwood, McClaren and even Bobby Robson were given the job, were they really the best English managers around? Most people expected Harry Redknapp to get the job ahead of Roy Hodgson. So how do their records compare?

Manager	Date	5-year Record	Win Pct	
Clough	1977	106-51-53	.626	better than Greenwood by 16.4%
Clough	1982	100-64-46	.629	better than Robson by 3.6%
Redknapp	2012	91-47-52	.603	better than Hodgson by 13.0%

The graphic above confirms what many people thought at the time. Brian Clough should have got the job in 1977. Managers improve their club Win Pct to their international one by an average of about 15%. So if Clough had improved his record at international level by, say 12% he would have had a win percentage for England of .750. Brian Clough was anything but average and, if he had taken advantage of Greenwood's weak opponents in the same way and improved by even 20% (not Greenwood's 26.8%), he would have reached .826 for England.

How would that have translated into results? It would have meant the equivalent of another five wins – enough to qualify for Argentina 78, sufficient to reach the final of Europa 80 and to reach at least the semi-final of Espana 82. The history of English football might have looked very different indeed.

So what have we learned? Mainly that a couple of managerial villains weren't actually that bad. Don Revie comes out of it very well, Steve McClaren less so, but, as we've seen elsewhere, Croatia have a better qualifying record than England and another manager would not necessarily have done much better with the players he had at his disposal.

We've seen that for all the heartbreak of Italia 90, Bobby Robson flattered to deceive and either side of 1966 Sir Alf was average at best. It took the FA a long time to employ a non-English manager but the two that have been installed so far have clearly produced everything but a trophy.

The Greatest Club Managers

Another straightforward question, and again one that is relatively easy to calculate. It would be very difficult though to compare club management levels in different countries and in different eras. This time I'll keep to league Win Pcts in England and total trophies won. So who has been the greatest English club manager of all?

In May 2000, *FourFourTwo* published the results of a survey given to managers in England and Scotland, asking for their top three all-time managers. The results had some interesting names in the mix. Who would have thought that John King and Jim Smith would make the list? This pair had performed wonders at lower levels but had never really been given the chance at a top club, and for this list I only wanted the best of the best. Most of the names I analysed were at the top of the survey too.

Below is the table of managers' Win Pcts in top flight English football:

Manager	Club	Years	W	D	L	Win Pct
Alex Ferguson	Man. Utd	1986-12	586	223	159	.715
Arsene Wenger	Arsenal	1996-12	333	141	96	.708
Don Revie	Leeds Utd	1961-74	237	110	73	.695
Bob Paisley	Liverpool	1974-83	212	99	67	.692
Kenny Dalglish	Liverpool	1985-12	240	106	84	.681
Bill Shankly	Liverpool	1962-74	260	129	115	.644
Matt Busby	Man. Utd	1946-71	470	241	255	.611
Herbert Chapman	Arsenal	1912-34	237	122	136	.600
Brian Clough	N. Forest	1967-93	371	183	240	.582
Bill Nicholson	Spurs	1959-74	274	156	178	.579
Stan Cullis	Wolves	1948-65	330	159	225	.574
Bobby Robson	Ipswich	1969-04	300	176	222	.556
Ron Greenwood	West Ham	1961-74	182	148	216	.469

Added for comparison, too few games to count:

Alf Ramsey	Ipswich	1961-78	52	28	46	.524
Jose Mourinho	Chelsea	2004-07	82	23	9	.820

Trophies won with English club sides only:

	European	League	FACup	LCup	Total
Alex Ferguson	3	12	5	4	24
Bob Paisley	4	6	0	3	13
Brian Clough	2	2	0	4	8
Bill Nicholson	2	1	3	2	8
Matt Busby	1	5	2	0	8
Arsene Wenger	0	3	4	0	7
Don Revie	2	2	1	1	6
Kenny Dalglish	0	4	2	1	7
Bill Shankly	1	3	2	0	6
Herbert Chapman	0	4	2	0	6
Stan Cullis	0	3	2	0	5
Bobby Robson	1	0	1	0	2
Ron Greenwood	1	0	1	0	2

PART 7: ENGLAND

"Obviously six points from four games is worth more than four points from four games so I'm not going to make myself a mathematical idiot."

– Roy Hodgson

I've already covered some aspects of the national team like managers, Peter Shilton, tournament football, Bobby Moore and Jack Charlton, but I feel there are still some areas that need tidying up. Did you know that England were worse defensively under Fabio Capello than they were under Steve McClaren? Well, you do now.

I'm also going to finally look at friendlies. It's been written elsewhere that England's form has been pretty constant through the last few decades but I don't agree with that. In regard to players I want to know if Wayne Rooney really is *that* important to the national side, whether Frank Lampard and Steven Gerrard can play in the same England side and if there are any referees that are more suited to England and vice-versa. How about England's greatest scorers? Is the list skewed by racking up lots of goals in friendlies?

England Managers – Cautious Or Cavalier?

Like dog owners and their dogs sometimes looking similar, a football team can take on some of the characteristics of its manager. Quiet and reserved, or vocal and gung-ho. Stereotypes come to the fore too. Would England under Kevin Keegan always be likely to go for the 4-3 win, would Fabio Capello's Italian background mean a stern defence for once? Here are the goals against averages (GAA) and goals scored averages (GSA) for England's managers in competitive matches:

	GAA
Bobby Robson	0.51
Glenn Hoddle	0.53
Steve McClaren	0.58
Terry Venables	0.60
Ron Greenwood	0.65
Sven-Goran Eriksson	0.68
Don Revie	0.70
Fabio Capello	0.73
Graham Taylor	0.74
Roy Hodgson	0.75
Alf Ramsey	0.88
Kevin Keegan	0.91
Walter Winterbottom	1.24

	GSA
Walter Winterbottom	2.62
Fabio Capello	2.45
Don Revie	2.20
Bobby Robson	2.09
Steve McClaren	2.00
Ron Greenwood	1.85
Sven-Goran Eriksson	1.82
Graham Taylor	1.79
Glenn Hoddle	1.73
Alf Ramsey	1.69
Terry Venables	1.60
Kevin Keegan	1.55
Roy Hodgson	1.25

So Glenn Hoddle and Steve McClaren are among the most defensive-minded of the managers, while Fabio Capello is one the most attack-minded of recent times. Bobby Robson proves how unlucky he was in the job as he is at or near to the top of each list. Roy Hodgson's position at the bottom of the GSA list will surely rise as he starts winning some qualifying matches, to leave Kevin Keegan as the worst attacking manager in post-war history. Now who would have predicted that?

Consistently Average?

Since winning the World Cup in 1966, has there ever really been a golden generation? A time when England were at any kind of peak or have they been a consistently good, but not great, team? As tables of such data are often misleading I've split the data into tables for competitive and friendly games:

Friendlies

	W	D	L	Win Pct
1950s	35	18	14	.657
1960s	46	10	18	.689
1970s	33	11	21	.592
1980s	31	14	17	.613
1990s	32	10	17	.627
21st C	30	14	16	.617

In friendly games, England have been fairly consistent, with the highest and lowest figures per decade only being around 9% apart. England have also played roughly the same amount of friendlies per decade except for the 1960s when they didn't have to qualify for either the 1966 or 1970 World Cup finals so played a few more. That was also the decade in which they were strongest. The second strongest friendly decade was the 1950s. Of the last three dates the 1990s were the best. These numbers don't correlate with the figures for competitive games at all:

Competitive record

	W	D	L	Win Pct	Best Progress
1950s	12	3	5	.675	
1960s	14	4	5	.696	won WC
1970s	23	7	6	.736	
1980s	27	18	7	.692	WC QF
1990s	24	20	6	.680	WC SF, ESF
21st C	52	15	11	.763	WC QF

Here the recent three decades see the 1990s as the weakest, the complete opposite to the friendlies table. The strongest competitive decade was actually the latest one, while the 1970s are next best, again in opposition to the previous table.

The combination of these two tables tends to even things out and give the mistaken impression that England were actually performing very steadily during these years.

Wayne Rooney – Talisman?

When Wayne Rooney was sent off during Euro 2012 qualifying and suspended for the first two games of the finals there was much talk about the impact of losing a 'world-class player'. Even though there was a chance that England could have been eliminated by the time he was eligible to play there was never really much question of leaving him at home. As it happened, although he scored against Ukraine, Rooney's play was generally poor. So is he really world class, and what impact does he have on the England team?

Competitive England Games:

	Pld	W	D	L	Win Pct
Without Rooney	18	12	2	4	.778
With Rooney	49	34	5	10	.796

Rooney has netted 21 competitive goals for England, good for a 0.43 goals per game strike rate, which is decent but nothing special at world-class level. It's more surprising, and depressing for England fans, that Rooney only improves the team by about 2% in competitive games. Add this to the fact that he has only scored once in the last ten tournament games he's played (and never at the World Cup) and it's clear that he has to start performing at the very top level very quickly if he's going to be any more than a minor footnote in international football history.

Tournament record:

	Pld	Gls
Euro 2004	2	4
WC 2006	4	0
WC 2010	4	0
Euro 2012	2	1

England's Real Top Scorers

Having looked at Wayne Rooney's competitive scoring record for England I thought I should take a trip through the all-time top scorers chart and see how it should really look. When Gary Lineker retired from international football he did so while being one goal behind Bobby Charlton in all England games. But when I decided to look at just the competitive goals for England would he actually come out on top?

England Players Scoring the Most Competitive Goals:

	Total Pld	Total Gls	Com. Pld	Com. Gls	GPG	Com. Pct.
M Owen	89	40	53	26	0.49	65%
G Lineker	80	48	40	22	0.55	46%
A Shearer	63	30	31	21	0.68	70%
W Rooney	76	29	49	21	0.43	72%
B Robson	90	26	43	15	0.35	58%
F Lampard	90	23	51	15	0.29	65%
B Charlton	106	49	29	14	0.48	29%
S Gerrard	96	19	58	14	0.24	74%
G Hurst	49	24	18	13	0.72	54%
K Keegan	63	21	27	13	0.48	62%
D Beckham	115	17	68	13	0.19	76%
D Platt	31	27	29	12	0.41	44%

For comparison:

N Lofthouse	33	30	4	6	1.50	20%
J Greaves	52	44	12	4	0.25	9%
T Finney	76	30	16	2	0.13	7%

Michael Owen moves to the top of the competitive goal total with 26, four ahead of Gary Lineker with Alan Shearer and Wayne Rooney close behind. Jimmy Greaves, with an overall total of 44 England goals, slips right down the list as he only managed four of them in competitive matches. Still-active players Frank Lampard and Steven Gerrard have a good chance to move up the list, especially as they both score a large portion of their goals in competitive games (65% and 74% respectively). Geoff Hurst has the best strike rate of the leading pack, averaging 0.72 goals per game.

Out On Their Feet – Are England Players Really That Tired?

Every generation thinks that the younger one has it easy compared to them. When I hear about players complaining about the long seasons I think back to the 1970s when at least the same number of games were played and with smaller squads. When England inevitably tumble out of a major tournament it's mentioned that they have a longer, harder season than the others, that the England players are burnt out. Is this backed up by the playing records?

I looked through all of England's qualifying games between 1974 and 2012 and split them into monthly segments to see if performance changed as the season progressed and the players supposedly tired. I further broke the games into 1974-1992 and 1992-2012 to see if there was any 'Premiership' effect.

	Pre-Premiership	Premiership
September	.583	.920
October	.833	.615
November	.778	.643
December	1.000	-
Pre-Christmas total	.784	.654
January	.500	-
February	1.000	.500
March	.750	.944
April	.750	.857
May	.643	.750
June	.800	.750
Post-Christmas total	.759	.817
All	.764	.768
Finals games	.519	.588

During both eras there are peaks and troughs on a monthly basis, but while the pre-Christmas and post-Christmas totals in the 1974-1992 period are fairly similar, the Premiership era has a large difference before and after Christmas. The strange thing is that rather than get worse as the season progresses, England are 16% better later in the season, so tiredness isn't an issue. But when finals games (in June and July) are highlighted the Win Pct drops by 18% in the recent years, but this isn't tiredness, it's just that England play better teams. That's why they lose more.

The Russian Linesman

In 1966, England's greatest moment happened largely because of a Russian linesman. When Geoff Hurst's extra time shot rebounded down from the underside of the bar, no one could be sure if the ball had crossed the line or not. All except the Russian linesman, who was in fact from Azerbaijan. Since then there have been various decisions that haven't gone England's way due to a Tunisian referee (with the Hand of God) and a Uruguayan referee (the Lampard no-goal). So my question is, are there any nationalities who have officiated when England win, or lose, more than others?

I've noticed that sometimes the TV pundits can be rather condescending towards officials of 'smaller' countries saying things like "the game was too big for him", as though they haven't undergone Fifa training and instruction.

In World Cup finals play, here is England's record against each continent:

	Win Pct
Europe	.613
South America	.600
CONCACAF	.500
Africa	.750
Other	1.000
TOTAL	.616

England have never won a World Cup game if the referee is from Argentina, Brazil, USA, Yugoslavia, Paraguay, Israel, Austria, Tunisia or Uruguay. In these games they have a combined record of five losses and eight draws, with a Win Pct of .308.

England's World Cup record when the referees are from:

	Win Pct
South America	.500
Europe	.657
Africa	.000
CONCACAF	.700
Other	.700

Overall England have a Win Pct of .657 with European referees and .550 with non-European referees.

Can You Play With Gerrard *And* Lampard?

A popular debate over the past decade, especially when England get knocked out of a tournament, is whether the national team can be successful playing two influential attack-minded midfielders in the same side. Steven Gerrard and Frank Lampard have been the mainstays of the England midfield for the past five tournaments, but do they work? The only way to check was to analyse the Win Pcts when one, the other or both played. Here are the figures for competitive games:

	W	D	L	Win Pct
Gerrard alone	14	4	2	.800
Lampard alone	7	1	1	.833
Lampard and Gerrard	22	6	4	.781

As you can see, there is hardly any difference between the three scenarios, so why the myth that England can't win with both of them? Maybe the influence of friendly games has grabbed the public imagination? So I looked at those too:

	W	D	L	Win Pct
Gerrard alone	10	3	2	.767
Lampard alone	3	3	4	.450
Lampard and Gerrard	13	6	6	.640

So in friendlies they do better when Gerrard plays alone than when they play together, but playing together is better than Lampard alone. Nothing in any of these figures suggests that there is any discernible problem caused by having both of them playing together, it's just another football myth.

PART 8: STOPPAGE TIME

"It's never over until it's over, but this is over!"

– Chris Kamara

It used to seem that during every FA Cup final there would be a mention of Wembley's pitch and its "wide open spaces" in the context of the players getting more tired than normal. After the re-build of the stadium, as recently as the 2012 League Cup final, Martin Keown was on the BBC talking about Wembley and its "massive pitch". I'm sure you can see where this is going.

Old Trafford, Eastlands, Ewood Park and Goodison Park all have larger playing surfaces than Wembley and 11 other Premiership grounds are within 5% of the pitch size. Hardly a great difference, is it?

Consistently Inconsistent

Earlier I explained how for many teams the awarding of penalties does not even out over a season, or even three seasons, so how balanced is the awarding of red and yellow cards? Does that even out over a season, or do some referees go to their pocket more often than others? Managers and players often say they just want consistency between referees but from the table below you can see they rarely get it.

Table of referees' card use over three Premiership seasons:

Referee	Games	Yellow	Red	YPG
Mike Dean	84	326	24	3.88
Mike Riley	74	273	12	3.69
Howard Webb	90	323	11	3.59
Steve Bennett	81	265	10	3.27
Lee Mason	35	114	7	3.26
Alan Wiley	88	272	6	3.09
Rob Styles	83	255	20	3.07
Phil Dowd	69	211	15	3.06
Martin Atkinson	76	232	11	3.05
Andre Marriner	46	139	9	3.02
Chris Foy	68	196	8	2.88
Peter Walton	66	185	5	2.80
Mark Halsey	78	152	8	1.95

YPG = Yellow cards per game

The Curious Case Of
Alex James

For younger readers, I just want to make clear that this section has nothing to do with the cheese-making, bass-playing member of Blur, but rather Alexander Wilson James, the Arsenal inside-forward of the 1930s. In some quarters James is considered the greatest player Arsenal have ever had, and based on his effect on the team it's hard to argue against. It was James who provided the ammunition for the likes of Cliff Bastin (128 league goals

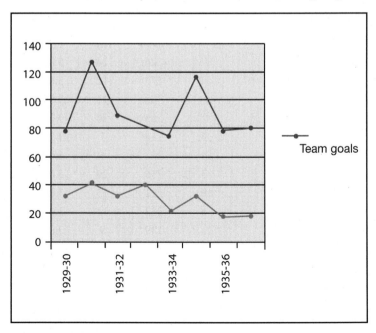

in 300 games, 1930-38) and Ted Drake (93 league goals in just 114 games, 1934-38).

Though James' goalscoring record for the Gunners is not exceptional (26 goals in 236 league appearances) his play-making was. It's a real shame that assists weren't recorded back then, and that newspaper reports weren't detailed enough, because his genius would have been easier to quantify, but what we do know is that when James played for Arsenal they scored more goals.

Two-thirds of Charity Shield/Community Shield winners are the league champions:

	Champions	Cup winners
1974-1992	10	4
1992-2011	12	7
Total	22	11

INDEX

A

B

C

E

F

G

H

Hodgson, Roy 214, 217-9, 225, 226-7
Holland 110-111, 128, 130, 135
Huddersfield Town 27-8, 29, 35, 124
Hughes, Mark 214
Hull City 27, 34, 49, 54, 96
Hungary 130

I

Ibrahimovic, Zlatan 120-122
Internazionale 43
Ipswich Town 28, 30, 32, 47, 48, 54, 87
Ireland 130
Israel 133
Italy 103, 130, 146-7

J

James, Alex 243
Jewell, Paul 77
Juventus 43, 71, 160

K

Kean, Steve 214
Keane, Robbie 174
Keane, Roy 112
Keegan, Kevin 217-9, 226-7, 232
Klinsmann, Jurgen 174
Klose, Miroslav 174
Koller, Jan 174

L

Lampard, Frank 228-9, 232
Lawrenson, Mark 74

N

Napoli 160, 161

Newcastle United 25, 27, 29, 48, 49, 61, 80, 96, 97, 100, 106, 110, 124

Nicholson, Bill 223

Northampton Town 35

Norway 130, 133

Norwich City 26

Nottingham Forest 25, 31, 32, 33, 34, 53, 70, 83, 116-7, 212

Notts County 35

O

Oldham Athletic 35, 46, 47, 82

Olympique Marseille 43

O'Neill, Martin 208, 214

Owen, Michael 232-3

Oxford United 35

P

Paisley, Bob 223

Paraguay 131, 132

Pardew, Alan 214

Pearce, Stuart 217

Pele 138, 175, 177

Peru 132

Perugia 43

Pirlo, Andrea 103

Platini, Michel 177

Plymouth Argyle 54

Poland 130

Polster, Toni 174

Porto 43
Portsmouth 29, 32, 34, 55-6, 96
Portugal 110-111, 130
Preston North End 54, 70, 82, 124
PSV 43

Q

Queens Park Rangers 26, 47, 53, 54, 63, 82

R

Ramsey, Sir Alf 217-9, 221, 226-7
Rangers 43
Raul 174
Reading 26, 49
Real Madrid 41, 43, 71, 160, 161, 183-5
Redknapp, Harry 157, 220
Revie, Don 56, 217-9, 223, 226-7
Rivaldo 175
Robson, Sir Bobby 217-9, 221, 223, 226-7
Romania 130
Romario 175
Ronaldo, Cristiano 103, 153, 173, 174
Rooney, Wayne 230-1, 232-3
Rosenborg 43
Rumenigge, Karl-Heinz 174
Russia 130

S

RB Salzburg 43
Scotland 130
Sevilla 160

V

W

Z